D0974563

Charles Finney

WOMEN OF FAITH SERIES

Amy Carmichael
Corrie ten Boom
Florence Nightingale
Gladys Aylward
Isobel Kuhn
Mary Slessor

MEN OF FAITH SERIES

Borden of Yale
Brother Andrew
C. S. Lewis
Charles Finney
Charles Spurgeon
Eric Liddell
George Muller
Hudson Taylor
Jim Elliot
Jonathan Goforth
John Hyde
John Wesley
Samuel Morris
Terry Waite
William Carey

John and Betty Stam

MEN OF FAITH

Charles Finney

Basil Miller

Official Biography for the Finney Sesquicentennial
Conference, Chicago 1942

BETHANY HOUSE PUBLISHERS
MINNEAPOLIS, MINNESOTA 55438
A Division of Bethany Fellowship, Inc.

Copyright MCMXLI by
Zondervan Publishing House

All rights reserved

ISBN 0-87123-061-5

Published by Bethany House Publishers
A Division of Bethany Fellowship, Inc.
6820 Auto Club Road, Minneapolis, Minnesota 55438

Printed in the United States of America

CONTENTS

CHAPTER I

YOUTH WITHOUT GOD

THE story of Charles G. Finney can be told in one word . . . *revivals*. This is the key that unlocks the treasures of his marvelous life. Even in his own thinking all else he did is worthy of note only in connection with his evangelism. It was he who sired a new evangelistic movement in America. He begins the story of his life by saying, "It has pleased God in some measure to connect my name and labors with an extensive movement of the church of Christ, regarded by some as a new era in its progress, especially in relation to revivals of religion."

So intense and distinctive was the soul-saving movement he brought into existence that some regarded him an innovator. But to Charles, the revivalist, slander, the impingment of his motives and all else concerned him little, if only he might *win precious souls to his Master*. For this he lived. Other items in his career were stacked on secondary shelves in his thinking with reference to this one thing.

After finishing the major part of his long and successful life he was asked to write his Memoirs when seventy-five. For thirty-one years he had theologized as a college teacher. For the same number of years he had pastored a college church. He had written many important and world-reaching books.

But in the telling of his story he tread upon this path of his career with a slight step that he might spot the light of interest wholly upon his part in winning men to the Christ. He forgot himself as a teacher . . . a theologian . . . a pastor. He passed over the many and varied avenues into which the influence of his striking personality had shot itself with vigor and spiritual dynamics.

He tuned his thinking to the soul-stirring themes of his revivals and lived over again in memory from the mellowing light of the three-quarter century mark of his life those glorious hours when under his ministry a half million souls yielded themselves to his Master's touch. Some called the book he wrote about himself his Autobiography. But to Charles himself the stories were memoirs . . . sacred memories hallowed with age of the times when heaven bent low to greet the souls of men.

And in the retelling of God's dealings with him and in retracing his dealings with lives immortal, this also is our emphasis. Other men stamped the imprint of their personalities upon immature students as teachers. Others challenged the world's intellect with their books. But in Charles Finney's thinking he was God's voice calling men to repentance. And his throne was not a lecture room in the colonnaded halls of learning.

He set his throne up in the inquiry room where men's souls were in the throes of eternal decision. It was here he fought his battles. This then shall be our journey. We will walk with him through those thrilling times when atmospheres were electrified with revival fires that the sparks of our own evangelism shall be kindled anew.

"I have kept no diary," he says, "and consequently must depend on my memory . . . The events I have witnessed in revivals of religion have made a very deep impression on my mind . . . I shall only sketch such an outline as will give a tolerably clear idea of the type which these revivals took on; and shall only relate a few of the particular instances of conversion which occurred in different places."

Finney played down in his own writing the events of his private life and gave attention to them only as they related to his evangelistic career. This dominate idea rode high at all times on the sea of his own thinking.

In the line of his ancestry the distant drums of the Revolutionary War roared and in the farther background of his people loomed the *Mayflower* in which an ancestor first landed in America. His father, Sylvester Finney, was a Revolutionary veteran who made his living as a farmer. On August 29, 1792, while the family was living at Warren in Litchfield County, Connecticut, Charles was born. Since Father Finney read the novels of one Richardson more than the Bible, he named his son after one of Richardson's fictitious characters, Charles Grandison.

His people were poor but *not* pious. Charles says he never heard prayer offered in his father's home until he himself offered it, nor did he read the Bible until he purchased one himself during the early weeks of his law practice in his twenty-ninth year.

The surge of empire rolled westward and the tide engulfed the unsettled Revolutionary veterans, so Father Finney along with neighbors loaded his ox wagons with possessions and cut a track through the wilderness to the unsettled beyond of the Hudson River. He stopped first at Brotherton and later moved to Hanover in Oneida County, New York. Here was to be Charles' boyhood home, "at that time, to a great extent, a wilderness," as Charles observes from the distant glance of seventy-three years later.

It was an outdoor life this future evangelist was to lead. There were farm chores to be performed, logs to be felled, soil to be tilled. When Charles was old enough he took down the long-barreled flintlock rifle which hung from deer antlers over the door and hied himself to the woods where such game as deer, turkey and wild pigeons were plentiful. He became an expert shot and hunting was a diversion he enjoyed throughout the more active years of his life.

Even at Oberlin when he was far beyond the half-century mark he would slip out to the edge of the settlement with his rifle and the ring of a shot told the neighbors that the famous teacher-evangelist would soon be around distributing to each a portion of the deer he had brought down.

His grandson builds for us a picture of the sturdy youth, thus, "When he was twenty he excelled every man and boy he met, in every specie of toil or sport. No man could throw him; no man could knock his hat off; no man could run faster, jump farther, leap higher or throw a ball with greater force and precision. When his family moved to the shore of Henderson's Bay, near Sackett's Harbor, he added to his accomplishments rowing, swimming and sailing."

True to the traditions of the New England pioneers the three R's were not neglected even in this wilderness. For the youth in their tomorrows must know how to read correctly, spell accurately, write legibly and to keep family accounts in order. The teachers usually boarded around among the families, staying at each place a week or so.

Such schools were the antecedents of the "little red school house," and in them Webster's blue-backed Speller, as well as Hodder's and Pike's Arithmetic, was to be found. The benches were crude that young Charles sat upon summer and winter each year until he was fifteen or sixteen, "and advanced so far as to be supposed capable of teaching a common school myself."

Close-by was the Hamilton Oneida Institute at Clinton, which Samuel Kirkland, a missionary to the Indians, had projected and named after Alexander Hamilton. This was to be the seed from which grew Hamilton College. Here Charles was a student for two years after he had advanced beyond the rural school stage.

Here his life was marked by the influence of Principal Seth Norton, striped by the Yale color. Norton, a classical scholar and a lover of music, inspired Charles with an ambition to secure a classical education and awakened a passion for music in the youth's heart.

"He taught him to sing," writes William Cochran, Finney's grandson, "to read music at sight and to play on the violin and . . . the violincello (or what we call the 'cello). That instrument appealed powerfully to Mr. Finney's passionate nature."

The first money Charles earned from his teaching went to buy a 'cello. In his spare hours he gave himself to the mastery of the instrument and a thorough study of harmony and musical composition, which soon developed the ability of investing an air with its appropriate chords and to write out the different parts of a chorus.

In Finney's later life this musical training was to step to the fore in his evangelism, for often the best musicians of the cities where he held his revivals conducted choirs for him.

"He had a musical voice of phenomenal range, flexibility and power," says Cochran in a memorial address on his grandfather, "and song was the natural expression of his healthy joyous soul. But he was also intensely emotional and almost as sensitive to sympathetic appeals as his 'cello was to the vibrations of the strings. It was not an unusual thing for him, strong and vigorous as he was, to weep over his 'cello."

This intensity of emotional outbursts, causing him often to feel deeply the surcharges of sentiment that played over an audience, was at the heart of his evangelistic appeals. And as he said his "sensibility often overflowed." But this overflow moved audiences and empowered his voice with spiritual energy.

When Charles was sixteen, in 1808, the family having moved to Henderson, New York, on Lake Ontario, he found a rural school in search of a master, and the next four years, summer bright and winter cold, he taught school. He became the idol of the pupils because he took part in their sports, always excelling them.

While school advantages were offered the youth, his religious influences were nil. "My parents were neither of them professors of religion," he affirms, "and I believe among our neighbors there were very few religious people. I seldom heard a sermon, unless it was an occasional one from some traveling preacher who would sometimes be found in that country. I recollect very well that the ignorance of the preachers that I heard was such that the people would return from meeting and spend a considerable time in irrepressible laughter at the strange mistakes . . . and absurdities which had been advanced."

Even when a church was about to be built in Oneida county the family hove farther into the heart of the wilderness and settled on the lake. "Here again I lived for several years, enjoying no better religious privileges than I had in Oneida county," he says.

The call of the War of 1812 sounded and Charles went to Sacket Harbor on the lake with the intention of enlisting in the navy, but here in one day he heard more profanity than he had heard in the twenty years of his life and it was more than he could stand. He was also accosted by a street woman, young and pretty.

His grandson says of the incident, "He looked at her in wonder and when he comprehended the nature of her request, he was so overcome with pity for her . . . that his cheeks burned, and before he could check it he was shedding tears . . . She, moved to shame, wept too." Fifty-five years later when relating the story, Finney remarked, "Oh, if I had only been a Christian at that time! That woman might have been saved! Perhaps God brought about this meeting on purpose to open her eyes and she may have repented."

There was thus to be no navy for Charles, doubtless a providence of God in throwing the lines of his life in another direction from which was to burst the glow of his spiritual awakening.

Shortly he returned to his native town, Warren, Connecticut, where he attended an academy for two years, during which time he supported himself by working on an uncle's farm, and conducting in the winter a singing school attended largely by the people from miles around.

At the academy he distinguished himself for leadership, acquired a reputation for wit and oratory in the literary society and served as editor of the hand-written school journal. He intended to go to Yale for a classical course, but his teacher persuaded him that Yale would be a waste of time since under his instruction it would be possible to complete the course in two instead of four years.

Charles spent the next two years in New Jersey teaching, and from time to time he returned to Warren to report the progress made in his classical studies and to receive further assignments. By this means he acquired a working knowledge of Latin, Greek and Hebrew, but in his Memoirs he looks with modesty upon these linguistic attainments, saying, "I never possessed so much knowledge of the ancient languages as to think myself capable of independently criticising our English translation of the Bible."

Looking back over this marvelous life, one wonders if the hand of God was not displayed in controlling the training of Mr. Finney for a career of evangelism. He later missed Princeton, as he now missed Yale, two schools which might have added little to his work in evangelism.

Four years later his teacher urged him to go South with him where they would establish an academy, but owing to his mother's illness he was persuaded to return home. Here again providence intervened, for around the bend in his career was to be law and law was to lead him to the Bible and the Bible . . . But this is running ahead of our story.

His parents, once Finney was home again, persuaded their son to enter the legal profession. At Adams, New

York, the law office of Judge Benjamin Wright, then a leading attorney in that part of the state, was opened to Charles, who was twenty-six years old, this being in 1818.

"Up to that time," he says in his Memoirs, "I had never enjoyed what might be called religious privileges. I had never lived in a praying community, except during the periods when I was attending the high school in New England; and the religion in that place was of a type not at all calculated to arrest my attention . . . I had never until this time lived where I could attend a stated prayer-meeting." Nor had he ever owned a Bible.

For two years he read law under Judge Wright after which he was admitted to the bar and taken into partnership. As a young attorney he took an interest in the civic activities of the community, and it was suggested that he join the Masons, which he did, thinking it would advance his status in the town.

"I was almost as ignorant of religion as a heathen," he affirms. "I had been brought up mostly in the woods. I had little regard to the Sabbath, and had no definite knowledge of religious truth."

In this spiritual condition the pastor of the local church, Rev. George W. Gale, a Princeton graduate and a preacher of no mean ability, invited Charles to lead the church choir. Gale's winning personality outdistanced his pulpit theology (as far as Charles was concerned), for his visits to the young lawyer's office meant more to Finney than his sermons.

He preached a hyper-Princetonian dogma that man's nature was totally incapable of any good and in the will there was no possibility of right choice. To him man's soul was entirely passive in regeneration, which within itself was a physical change. If he preached on repentance, he was sure to inform the congregation that repentance was impossible, or if speaking on saving faith, he would tell his listeners that until grace through the Holy Spirit had changed their natures they could not believe.

Finding many references in his legal books to the Mosaic code of laws as well as other Biblical passages, Finney decided to buy a Bible that he might check the references and read it at leisure. He found Gale's hyperdogmatic positions not squaring themselves with the Bible and he told the minister so.

"In conversing with him," states the lawyer, " and asking him questions, I perceived that his own mind was . . . mystified; and that he did not accurately define to himself what he meant by many of the important terms that he used . . . We had a great many interesting conversations; but they seemed rather to stimulate my own mind to inquiry than to satisfy me in respect to the truth."

He attended prayer meeting regularly but the praying did little to turn his attention to religion, for the church's *praying was not followed by receiving.* The lawyer chided the praying preacher for his non-receiving. "I heard them pray continually for the outpouring of the Holy Spirit, and as often confess that they did not receive what they asked for," he says.

Their confession, that praying often for a revival they secured none, seemed so inconsistent to Charles that once in a prayer meeting, when asked if he wanted to be prayed for, the choir-leading lawyer stood up and said, "I suppose that I need to be prayed for . . . but I do not see that it would do any good for you to pray for me; for you are continually asking, but you do not receive. You have been praying for a revival of religion ever since I have been in Adams, and yet you have it not."

Once he told them, "You have prayed enough since I have attended these meetings to have prayed the devil out of Adams if there is any virtue to your praying."

He could out-argue their prayers but could not refute the call the Bible made to his soul while reading it in the privacy of his office. "But on further reading of my Bible it struck me . . . they did not pray in faith . . . And after struggling in that way my mind became settled that . . . the Bible was, nevertheless, the word of God."

This settled, God's battle for his soul was won.

Chapter II

THE ALTAR IN THE WOODS

In spite of the minister's doubts as to whether or not his choir leader would be saved, a band of the young people of the church decided to pray for Charles' conversion. Among the group was the young lady who was later to become his wife. These prayer meetings went on seriously for some time until they reached their climax on Sunday evening, October 7, 1821, when Charles was twenty-nine.

For sometime previous to this he had been a questing disciple though not openly. He was numbered among those who would seek at night or in the closets of his own mind when from the gaze of all others his innermost thoughts and longings were locked securely.

Little is known about church that night, the power of the minister's discourse, his theme, but Charles says about that evening, "I made up my mind that I would settle the question of my soul's salvation at once, that if it were possible I would make peace with God."

Providence opened the way that on the following Monday and Tuesday little business came into the office so Charles could have time to seek the Lord. "But as providence would have it," he says, "I was not much occupied either on Monday or Tuesday; and had opportunity to read my Bible and engage in prayer most of the time."

His proud heart broke through the thin shell of his resolution when reading and praying time came. He didn't want anyone to know he was seeking the Lord. Until that time he had laid his Bible openly on the table so his clients could see it. Now, however, he was ashamed to be seen reading it. So whenever he heard a client's feet padding toward his room he hid the Book, or if one came in unexpectedly he carelessly threw law books over the Bible, "to create the impression that I had not had it in hand."

"I did not want to see my minister," he declares, "because I did not want to let him know how I felt, and I had no confidence that he would understand my case, and give me the direction I needed."

And he was off the elders of the church for the same reason, nor did he want to talk to any professed Christians.

But he must pray to relieve the burden that was burning its way through the surface of his spiritual indifference. So he plugged the keyhole of his office door that his whispered prayers could not be heard outside.

Praying behind plugged keyholes or whispering his way to God's throne or shame-facedly reading from the Word God's instructions for penitent sinners, did not relieve the pent-up tensions of his soul. "My convictions increased," he says, "but still it seemed as if my heart grew harder. I could not shed a tear; I could not pray. I had no opportunity to pray above my breath."

He endeavored to seek the Lord's face in such a sly, off-handed manner as to arouse no suspicion among others that he was a sin-weary prodigal searching for the road that leads to Father's home. This only added to his spiritual unrest.

"Tuesday night I had become very nervous; and in the night a strange feeling came over me as if I was about to die. I knew that if I did I should sink down into hell." He was as a man whose eyes had been hell-bound in their seeing and when God's glorious light did break across the dark hills of his soul, he could tell others about the burning pit with such vividness that they sought to flee its wrath.

The messages God had for him to proclaim were now in the brewing crucible of his own experience.

Came the dawn of Wednesday after a wakeful night of conviction, and on the prodigal's way to his office for a session with Blackstone an inner voice confronted him, saying, "What are you waiting for? . . . Are you endeavoring to work out a righteousness of your own?"

His spiritual eyes were opened and he beheld the reality and fullness of Christ's atonement. "I saw that His work was a finished work; and that instead of having or needing any righteousness of my own to recommend me to God, I had to submit myself to . . . Christ. Gospel salvation seemed to me to be an offer of something to be accepted . . . and that all was necessary on my part was to get my own consent to give up my sins and accept Christ."

Came the Voice, "Will you accept it now, today?"

Answered Charles, "Yes, I will accept it today or will die in the attempt."

North of the village lay a woods where he accustomedly walked during pleasant weather. And as he neared the office his storm-torn soul drove him to the timbers. Somewhere out there he knew he must find an altar where his voice could be freed from fear and his piled-up emotions could be drained from the reservoir of his being.

His sessions with Blackstone seeking legal loopholes for semi-honest clients were over though he knew it not. For him that day the office was closed. The Spirit drove him into the wilderness to pray. About a quarter of a mile from the road he went deep into the woods so none could see nor hear.

"I . . . found a place where some large trees had fallen across each other, leaving an opening between. There I saw I could make a kind of closet. I crept into this place and knelt down for prayer."

Finding his prayer closet he recalled the promise he made as he climbed the hill into the woods, "I will give my heart to God or I never will come down from there."

But his heart was so chilled that he could not pray and when he tried he became dumb. He tells it thus, "I had nothing to say to God . . . In attempting to pray I would hear a rustling in the leaves . . . and would stop and look up to see if somebody were not coming."

Conviction verged him toward the brink of despair. "When I came to try, I found I could not give my heart to God. My inner soul hung back . . . I began to feel deeply that it was too late . . . that I was given up of God and was past hope."

Flashes out of his memory threw reassuring passages from the Bible at him. "I knew that it was God's Word and God's voice . . . that spoke to me," he says describing those scenes. "The Spirit seemed to lay stress upon the idea in the text, 'When you search for me with all your heart.' I told the Lord that I would take Him at His word; that He could not lie; and that therefore I was sure that He heard my prayer . . . "

Struggling through the maze of his own sins back to God he clung to those promises as they leaped into his mind. Then he prayed as he says, "till my mind became so full that before I was aware of it I was on my feet and tripping up the ascent toward the road. The question of my being converted had not so much as arisen to my thought . . . I recollect saying with great emphasis, 'If I am ever converted I will preach the Gospel.'"

Out on the road peace quieted the tempest which tossed his thoughts like anchorless barges on the sea of his mind. "So perfectly quiet," he avows, "was my mind that it seemed as if all nature listened."

He had prayed from early morning until noon unconscious of the passing time. And as he walked "all sense of sin, all consciousness of present sin or guilt had departed from me . . . The repose of my mind was unspeakably great . . . and the most profound spiritual tranquility had taken full possession of me."

He went to dinner only to find that his soul which had fed on the Bread of heaven had driven appetite for food from his physical body. Judge Wright was gone to dinner, so Charles now made spiritually new, took down his 'cello and played a sacred piece. And as he sang tears welled from the deep springs of his being. "I could not hear my own voice in singing without causing my sensibility to overflow," he testifies. "There was a great sweetness and tenderness in my thoughts and feelings."

As dusk darkened his law office and the Judge bid him good night, Charles was Spirit-driven into the back room to pray. Few records of conversions and Spirit-baptisms equal the experience he was about to go through on wings of joy as he entered the rear room. Let's go into that inner sanctuary through his own description:

"There was . . . no light in the room; nevertheless it appeared to me as if it were perfectly light. As I went in and shut the door . . . it seemed as if I met the Lord Jesus Christ face to face . . . as I would see any other man. He said nothing, but looked at me in such a manner as to break me right down at His feet . . . it seemed to me a reality that He stood before me and I fell down at His feet and poured out my soul to Him. I wept like a child . . . I bathed His feet with my tears."

This state continued for some time yet Mr. Finney could recollect nothing he said, but when he broke the interview, as he calls it, and returned to the inner office the fire had long since burned down. Nor was the surcharging of his soul with a mighty baptism completed. He goes on to describe the after-effects of meeting Christ face to face:

"But as I turned and was about to take a seat by the fire I received a mighty baptism of the Holy Ghost. Without expecting it . . . the Holy Spirit descended upon me in a manner that seemed to go through me body and soul. I could feel the impression like a wave of electricity going through and through me. Indeed it seemed to come in waves and waves of liquid love . . . like the very breath of God . . . it seemed to fan me like immense wings.

"No words can express the wonderful love that was shed abroad in my heart. I wept aloud with joy and love; and . . . I bellowed out the unutterable gushings of my heart. These waves came over me and over me and over me one after the other until I recollect I cried out, 'I shall die if these waves continue to pass over me . . . Lord, I cannot bear any more.'"

Yet he was calm, for he says, "I had no fear of death."

In this mental state the doctrine of justification by faith as a present experience was taught him of God. "I could now see and undersand what was meant by the passage, 'Being justified by faith, we have peace with God . . .' I could see that the moment I believed while up in the woods all sense of condemnation had entirely dropped out of my mind; and from that moment I could not feel a sense of guilt or condemnation . . . My sense of guilt was gone; my sins were gone . . . I felt justified by faith . . . I was in a state in which I did not sin. My heart was so full of love that it ran over."

Chapter III

PLEADING CHRIST'S CAUSE

On that day the life career of Charles Finney was launched. He closed his law books forever and opened his Bible. From then on he had a retainer to plead the cause of his Master and the squabbles of others no longer enticed him to the fleshpots of the law courts.

He no more was a partner of Judge (or Squire as he calls him) Wright for he had become a joint-heir with Christ, and all legal bonds binding him to an earthly partnership were dissolved.

"Finney was the instrument God wanted," writes A. M. Hills in his Finney biography, "and He used His sovereign right to deal with him spirtually after an unusual manner, and equip him at once for a matchless service."

Doubtless in the literature of spiritual pilgrimages there is no parallel to such a soul baptism being received along with conversion as Finney's. It was God's method of fitting him to sire an evangelistic movement for the modern age.

Charles' salvation work began at once. Late that Wednesday evening a member of the choir came to his office and on seeing the lawyer weeping, he asked, "Mr. Finney, what ails you? Are you in pain?"

"No, but so happy that I cannot live," came Charles' answer.

Rushing out of the office the visitor found an elder of the church and brought him to see the lawyer. Then a third friend came in and listened to Charles' marvelous testimony. Falling to the floor he cried, "Do pray for me," soon to be converted.

"This morning (Thursday) I went down into the office and there was having a renewal of these mighty waves of love and salvation overflowing me, when Squire Wright came into the office. I said a few words to him on the subject of salvation . . . He dropped his head . . . I thought no more of it then, but afterward found that the remark I made pierced him like a sword; and he did not recover from it till he was converted," says Mr. Finney in delineating the beginnings of his soul-reaching work.

Receiving such a heaven-filled baptism, he was not content until others knew the glory of seeing his Lord and Savior. He told it wherever he went and to all passers on his life's road, which to him had become Isaiah's highway of holiness.

"Mr. Finney," said Deacon B——who came into the office that morning, "do you recollect that my cause is to be tried at ten o'clock this morning? I suppose you are ready?"

"Deacon," came Finney's memorable answer, "I have a retainer from the Lord Jesus Christ to plead His cause and I cannot plead yours."

Looking at Charles with astonishment the good deacon, somewhat low in spiritual status, replied, "What do you mean?"

"I told him in a few words," writes Mr. Finney, "that I had enlisted in the cause of Christ; and then repeated that I had a retainer from the Lord Jesus Christ to plead His cause, and that he must go and get somebody else to attend his law suit: I could not do it."

So shocked was the churchman that his head dropped on his chest and slowly he walked to the middle of the street, where Finney saw him in deep meditation. Immediately he went to the party whom he was suing and settled the suit. "He then betook himself to prayer," says Charles, "and soon got into a much higher religious state than he had ever been in before."

Nor could he remain seated in his office waiting for people to whom he might talk about their spiritual welfare. "I soon sallied forth from the office," he says, "to converse with those whom I should meet about their souls. I had the impression . . . that God wanted me to preach the Gospel, and that I must begin immediately. I somehow seemed to know it . . . with a certainty that was past all possibility of doubt."

When first convicted, he states, he faced the possibility of having to give up his legal practie. "This at first stumbled me . . . but now after receiving these baptisms of the Spirit I was quite willing to preach the Gospel. Nay, I found that I was unwilling to do anything else. I had no longer any desire to practice law . . . I had no disposition to make money. I had no hungering and thirsting after worldly pleasures and amusements in any direction . . . Nothing, it seemed, could be put in competition with the worth of souls; and no labor . . . could be so sweet . . . as that of holding up Christ to a dying world."

With this divinely inwrought feeling of woe-is-me-if-I-preach-not-the-Gospel, he went forth to talk with whom he might meet. First he went to the shoemaker's shop where a young man was defending Universalism, and Charles being prepared by the Spirit gave answer. The young man walked out of the shop, "climbed over the fence and was steering straight across the fields toward the woods." He did not return until he had found Finney's transforming experience of grace.

At evening he called at the home of a friend and on being asked to say grace over tea, Charles became so agitated about the unsaved condition of two young people at the table that he began to weep. The young man rushed from the table and locked himself in a near-by room, "and was not seen again till the next morning, when he came out expressing a blessed hope in Christ. He has been for many years an able minister of the Gospel."

And of course excitement in the village ran high. Some said one thing about Finney's experience and some quite another. They asked, "Is he sincere? Is he mentally unbalanced?" One declared, "It's a hoax. He is simply trying to see what he can make Christian people believe."

Gale had been right in declaring, "Some of the young people will never be converted before Finney is." And he expressed doubts shortly before that Charles could be won by the church's praying folk.

The young people were taking refuge from Gale's gospelizing behind the lawyer's skirts. Said one man to his pious wife, "If religion is true, why don't you convert Finney? If you can convert Finney, I will believe in religion."

That night with common consent, no announcement having been made, the villagers crowded into the church. Finney was there as also was the minister. Charles says about that service, "No one seemed ready to open the meeting; but the house was packed to its utmost. I did not wait for anybody, but arose and began by saying that I then knew religion was from God . . ."

He testified to what he had received, and his experience brought a confession from the minister, saying, "I believe I have been in the way of the church and I have discouraged the church when they proposed to pray for Mr. Finney. And when I heard that he was converted I had no faith, I did not believe it."

Then Charles appointed a meeting for the youth of the church, whom one by one he was shortly to see converted, "and the work continued among them until but one of their number was left unconverted."

Such a noble work could not be confined to Adams but it spread to other villages where conversions were regularly reported. Charles spoke to all classes. To the night meetings was added a morning prayer meeting. The word of God had a wonderful power, cutting through hardened souls.

Then Mr. Finney felt led to visit his family at Henderson, where his father met him at the gate of his home. "How do you do, Charles?" asked his father.

"I am well, father, body and soul," he replied. "But, father, you are an old man; all your children are grown up and have left your home, and I never heard a prayer in my father's house."

"I know it, Charles, come in and pray yourself."

In the son went for prayer, shortly to see both father and mother genuinely brought to the Lord. For two or three days Charles remained in the community talking freely with people about their souls. Soon the glory broke and in the Congregational Church the heavenly fire fell. Said Charles' brother who was present at the meeting. "The brothers and sisters that were on their knees began to groan and sigh and weep and agonize in prayer. The deacon (who was leading the prayer) continued to struggle . . . and when he ceased no one in the room could get off of their knees. They could only weep and confess and all melt down before the Lord."

From the meeting God's work spread in every direction over the town. "And thus," relates Mr. Finney, "it spread from Adams as a center throughout nearly all the towns in the county."

Later when conversion's power struck Squire Wright's soul he was over in the valley beyond the woods where Finney had been converted. "He paced to and fro, singing as loudly as he could sing . . . clap his hands . . . stop and shout and clap his hands." And when he came back to town he cried, "I've got it! I've got it!"

Finney felt so strangely out of place among the Masons after these meetings that he withdrew from their fellowship. He was launched upon an evangelistic career from which there was no turning.

"About as much mystery," says G. Fredrick Wright, "hangs over the first year and a half of Finney's life subsequent to his conversion as that which shrouds the corresponding period of the Apostle Paul's renewed life."

He was now ready to work for his Redeemer. Nature had endowed him with many valuable qualifications for spiritual labors. His physique was strong, his movements were graceful, his appearance, dominating. His voice was clear and possessed of a rare flexibility. Even at old age he was able to sing solos. His mannerisms in speech were few and his intonations were as near perfect as possible. Combined with these facilities was a brilliant and logical mind.

Living as a pioneer his character had been rounded out by the building of a mental and physical independence that was to send him far in God's work.

"In the spring of this year, 1822," he says, "I put myself under the care of the Presbytery as a candidate for the Gospel ministry. Some of the ministers urged me to go to Princeton to study theology, but I declined."

When asked why he refused to go, he answered, "Pecuniary circumstances forbid it." In reply the brethren asked. "If your expenses are paid, will you go?" "No . . ."

Then the truth was out. "I plainly told them," he says, at length cornered for the underlying reason, "that I would not put myself under such an influence as they had been under; that I was confident they had been wrongly educated, that they were not ministers that met my ideal . . ."

Such indeed must have been shocking to the ministerial leaders, but shocking or no, Finney would have nothing of that training which had taken their spiritual zeal from them. "So they appointed my pastor to superintend my studies," he goes on to note. "But my studies, so far as he was concerned as my teacher, were little else than controversy."

Mr. Gale's dogmas were old-schooled, harsh and repellent to Finney. His views of original sin and man's inability to seek redemption were so strict that the new convert could see no experiential basis for them. So overboard he threw the reverend's theological tenets.

"These doctrines," the babe in theology affirms, "I could not receive. I could not accept his views on the subject of atonement, regeneration, faith, repentance, the slavery of the will, or any of the kindred doctrines . . . I was, however, but a child in theology and a novice in religion and Biblical learning; but I thought he did not sustain his views from the Bible and told him so."

Finney's logical mind drove his thinking back to the Bible as the true foundation of doctrine. "I asked him," he affirms, "if the Bible did not require all to believe and be saved."

Replied Mr. Gale, "Mr. Finney, if you continue to argue and reason, you will land in infidelity . . . You must not be so opinionated, but accept the teachings of the great doctors of the church."

As a student of law Finney had been trained in exact thinking, and he was not willing to abdicate reason from its throne to suit the ready-made theology the doctors of the church held out to him. He prefaced his *Systematic Theology* twenty years later by saying: "You were made to think . . . to develop your powers of study. God designed that religion should require thought . . ." And thinking upon the Bible basis to him was to be the foundation of theological science.

"Often when I left Mr. Gale," he says, "I would go to my room and spend a long time on my knees over my Bible. Indeed I read my Bible on my knees a great deal during those days . . . beseeching the Lord to teach me His own mind . . . I had no where to go but directly to the Bible . . ." And here he laid the groundwork for all his evangelistic appeals. From henceforth, whether confronting individuals with the Gospel, preaching to multitudes or teaching in the lecture room, he was an evangelist whose dogmas were the heart of the Bible thrown at men's souls.

On other points of ministerial practice he diverged from the views of Mr. Gale. He says, "I found his views to be almost the reverse of those which I entertained on all such practical questions relating to my duty as a minister."

Gale said, "Write and read your sermons . . ." Finney retorted, "What would be thought of a lawyer who should stand up before a jury and read an essay to them? He would lose his case!"

Winning the case, when pleading Christ's cause, was the end of the sermon, and not merely the effect of one's polished Gospel essay. "I talked to the people," Mr. Finney asserts, "as I would have talked to a jury. Of all the causes that were ever plead, the cause of religion, I thought, had the fewest able advocates, and that if advocates at the bar should pursue the same course in pleading the cause of their clients that ministers do in pleading the cause of Christ with sinners, they would not gain a single case."

Those who heard him preach often said, "It seemed as if Mr. Finney had taken me alone and was conversing with me face to face."

His style of preparation was as he went among the people "to learn their wants. Then in light of the Holy Spirit I take the subject that I think will meet their present necessities . . . I pray much over the subject and then go and pour it out to the people."

His work was so contrary to that of his teacher that Mr. Gale said, "Mr. Finney, I shall be very much ashamed to have it known, wherever you go, that you have studied theology with me." And Finney "held down his head and felt discouraged." From this viewpoint Mr. Gale later relented and became very proud of his evangelistic student. He even went so far as to soften his theological views and adopt those somewhat similar to Finney's.

"His sermons," writes Beardsley, "which he delivered with such power he never regarded as the products of his own brain." Finney said of them, "If I did not preach from inspiration, I don't know how I did preach."

At length after this unusual course of ministerial preparation, Finney was licensed to preach by the Presbytery on December 30, 1823, having spent a year and a half out-arguing his tutor and explicitly tuning his thinking to the Spirit's instruction.

He was given two texts from which he preached two trial sermons before the ministers. Expecting opposition because of his new doctrinal positions, he was surprised when the vote for license was unanimous. Professor Wright, his first biographer, thinks this was due not to love of the ministers for Finney or his views "but to general considerations of policy, and from fear of being found fighting against God."

The key to Finney's early ministry as well as to his evangelistic success is to be found in "the baptism of the Holy Ghost, which is indispensable to ministerial success." Of this he writes:

"When Christ commissioned His apostles to . . . preach, He told them to abide at Jerusalem till they were endued with power from on high. This power . . . was the baptism of the Holy Ghost poured out upon them . . . This was an indispensable qualification for success in their ministry . . . Without the direct teaching of the Holy Spirit, a man will never make much progress in preaching the Gospel."

Dr. A. M. Hills, who studied under Finney at Oberlin, says of his matchless ministry ". . . our mind goes back to the college days when we heard Finney, and felt again the thrill of his overpowering eloquence. We thought him then to be the prince of preachers and evangelists; a judgment we have never reversed. He was . . . a man of nature and of the desert, unspoiled by society, and untrammeled by the . . . regulations of the schools, but taught of God and filled with the Holy Ghost. *God had His giant at last.*"

He was fitted now, after his license, to take up God's cause in earnest. The Bible was his chief textbook, the Holy Spirit his teacher, prayer his strength, and he was prepared to go forth declaring that others might receive the marvelous experience which he possessed. Grounded in a know-so redemption, he proclaimed to others they too might have the divine witness that they had been born anew.

God's man was now ready for God's appointed task and soon a door of opportunity was to open into which Charles was to step — an open door leading into grand tomorrows of soul winning.

CHAPTER IV

LAUNCHING FORTH IN EVANGELISM

Probably no minister went forth into his life's career with less expectation of success and of a brilliant future than Charles Finney. He felt he was handicapped by lack of proper ministerial training. He determined to be God-taught even though his man-teaching was lacking. So he set out for the less privileged places with his Gospel message.

"Having had no regular training for the ministry," he says, "I did not expect or desire to labor in large towns or cities or minister to cultivated congregations. I intended to go into the new settlements and preach in schoolhouses and barns and groves as best I could."

Accordingly after receiving his license to preach he took a commission from the Female Missionary Society, Western District of New York, which was located in Oneida county. His term of service was to have been three months, and the region in Jefferson county at Evans Mills and Antwerp, two villages which were about thirteen miles apart. He aimed to divide his Sundays between the two places, where there were two churches, one a Congregational without a minister and the other a Baptist with a minister.

"I presented my credentials to the deacons of the church," he says in describing his launching forth into God's work. "They were glad to see me . . . They had no meeting house; but the two churches worshipped alternately in a large stone schoolhouse." Due to this fact he could work at Evans Mills only on those Sundays when the Congregationalists held forth, so this necessitated his going to Antwerp on the other Sundays, though every night he was free to preach at his first appointment.

The tide of religious conditions ebbed low. He says in a letter, "The church was disheartened and hung their harps upon the willows. The dear Zion was robed in mourning . . . Rebellion against the blessed God, under almost every form and in every shocking degree stalked aboard with unblushing front . . . The streets sounded with impious oaths . . . My soul was sick and I commenced my labors amongst them with plain dealings and denounced the terrors of the Almighty against them for their impious wickedness and ruinous rejection of the gospel of God's dear Son."

His preaching at Evans Mills attracted attention from the start, for he reasoned with men about their souls and confronted them with a transforming Gospel, though no visible results appeared. So one Sunday evening he told the congregation that he was dissatisfied with their rejection of the Gospel.

Reading the signs of the Spirit's directions, he said, "Now I must know your minds, and I want all of you who will give your pledge to make your peace with God immediately, to rise up; but all of you who are resolved not to become Christians and wish me to understand so and Christ to understand so, remain sitting."

This shocked the congregation which had often complimented the preacher upon his various messages. "They looked at one another and at me, and all sat still, just as I expected." He spoke again, "Then you are committed. You have taken your stand. You have rejected Christ and His Gospel . . . You may remember as long as you live that you have thus publicly committed yourselves against the Savior."

The congregation stalked from the building in a huff. What few religious professors there were in the audience hung their heads in shame. Only a good Baptist deacon caught the Spirit's warnings and said, "Brother Finney, you have got them. They cannot rest under this and you will see results." So together the two agreed to spend the next day in fasting and prayer, a policy Finney always followed when spiritual results were not forthcoming in his revivals.

They prayed separately in the morning; together in the afternoon. And while the two prayed the townsfolk went about in an uprising of indignation at the insulting remarks of the new minister. "Just at evening the Lord gave us great enlargement," he says concerning that prayer meeting in the woods where he and the deacon had prevailed throughout the afternoon, "and promise of victory. Both of us felt assured that we had prevailed with God; and that the power of God would be revealed among the people."

Finney believed that nothing could be effected in a revival except through prayer and by the Spirit's special aid. So here, as in all his subsequent revivals, he secured united prayer for the Spirit's engulfment.

As he and the deacon came from their prayer closet in the woods they found the meeting house packed. Charles had taken no thought as to what he should preach, of which fact he says, "this was common with me at that time." The Spirit gave him the text, "Say ye to the righteous that it shall be well with him . . . Woe to the wicked! it shall be ill with him."

"The Spirit of God came upon me with such power," he remarks, "that it was like opening a battery upon them . . . The word of God came through me in a manner that I could see was carrying all before it. It was a fire and a hammer breaking the rock."

The effect was electric, and he dismissed the congregation without giving a chance to pray. One woman fell under the Spirit's power, but Finney didn't linger behind. Instead of going to the home where he had been staying, he went to another place without telling the family he had been with each night. Consequently throughout the night person after person sent for the evangelist to come and pray for them. But Finney could not be found.

One man, who had opposed the revival, was struck with apoplexy, and when informed by the doctor that he was dying, he stammered, "Don't let Finney pray over my corpse." "This," as Mr. Finney states, "was the last of the opposition in that place."

There were great outbursts of emotionalism during these meetings. One woman fell speechless and lay in a trance for sixteen hours, "emerging with a song of deliverance upon her lips." One man came to church armed to kill Finney and during the sermon he fell from his seat, crying, "I am sinking into hell." Even the strongest nerved men were swept before the Spirit's power to be rendered so weak that friends carried them home.

Here Finney formed a lasting friendship with a minister named Father Nash, whom he had met first at the Presbytery where he had been licensed. Since then Nash had suffered a breakdown due to inflamed eyes, consequently he gave himself wholly to prayer.

"He had a terrible overhauling," as the revivalist says it, "in his whole Christian experience."

When he came to Evans Mills he was full of the power of prayer, and an altogether different man from what he had been when Finney first met him. Father Nash kept a "praying list," as he termed it, of the names of persons whom he made subjects of prayer each day. "And praying with him," affirms Mr. Finney, "and hearing him pray in meeting, I found that his gift of prayer was wonderful and his faith almost miraculous." Through their years of laboring together, often Father Nash would not even attend meetings, and while Finney was preaching Nash was praying for the Spirit's outpouring upon him.

In the town was a notorious tavern keeper, "whose house was the resort of all the opposers of the revival." Preacher and prayer put him on the prayer list, and one night the man came to church as the folk thought to make a disturbance. Some people got up and left, afraid of what he might do.

Let Finney tell the story: "He sat and writhed upon his seat and was very uneasy. He soon arose and tremblingly asked me if he might say a few words . . . and proceeded to make one of the most heart-broken confessions that I almost ever heard . . . he soon came out and professed a hope, abolished all the revelry and profanity and from that time . . . a prayer meeting was held in his bar-room nearly every night."

Near Evans Mills was a German community where Finney was invited to preach. Taking the text, "Without holiness no man shall see the Lord," he began to explain what holiness of heart and life was to these folk who could not understand English very well. Conviction swept the entire community and "the revival resulted in the conversion of the whole church . . . and of nearly the whole community of Germans. It was one of the most interesting revivals I ever witnessed."

Both churches at Evans Mills and Antwerp were so strengthened by the revivals that they each built commodious stone meeting houses and as Finney affirms "have had a healthy state of religion there since that time."

On July 1, 1824, during the time of the revival, the St. Lawrence Presbytery met at Evans Mills and considered the advisibility of ordaining this preacher upon whom God's seal of ordination had already been stamped. One brother suggested that since the people had come together to hear Mr. Finney preach, why not hear him now. Finney thought this good brother wanted to see what he could do on a moment's notice. So the revivalist arose and taking his text, "Without holiness no man shall see the Lord," proceeded to give the brethren a serious-minded sermon on the results of spiritual holiness.

Thus the service of ordination took place. In his Memoirs Finney passes it over with a sentence. "The Presbytery were called together to ordain me, *which they did.*" It was a higher seal he sought on his life for soul winning . . . the seal of the Holy Spirit, which consciously he labored always to have upon him when he arose to proclaim "the unsearchable riches of Christ."

When Mr. Finney first undertook these labors he was weak in body, even his lungs being so affected that he coughed blood, and it was thought he could not live long. Mr. Gale cautioned him to preach but once a week and not more than a half hour at a time. But at the end of his missionary labors during those six months, which time he preached once a day, his health was restored, his lungs were sound and he preached without even the slightest fatigue, many of those sermons running for a two-hour stretch.

He says, "I preached out of doors; I preached in barns; I preached in schoolhouses; and a glorious revival spread over that region of country."

Many of his ministerial brethren accused him of letting down the dignity of the pulpit, but Finney retorted, "When I come to preach the Gospel, I am so anxious to be thoroughly understood that I study in the most earnest manner . . . to express my thoughts with the greatest simplicity of language."

When ministers asked, "Why don't you illustrate from events of ancient history?" he replied, "My object is not to cultivate a style of oratory that should soar above the heads of the people . . . and I use any language adapted to this end."

When ministers urged him to preach as they did, he said, "Show me a more excellent way. Show me the fruits of your ministry, and if they so far exceed mine as to give me evidence that you have found a more excellent way, I will adopt your views . . . I never can adopt your manner of preaching the Gospel until I have higher evidence that you are right and I am wrong."

When he went over to Antwerp, after the Evans Mills revival had run it course, he found the church key in the custodianship of a tavern keeper, who refused to open the building. So the meeting was transferred to the schoolhouse. But God's man gave himself to prayer and though "the atmosphere seemed to be poison," God's answer came in the words, "Be not afraid . . .

for I am with thee . . . For I have much people in this city."

That Sunday morning Mr. Finney arose early and went into the woods, for he realized he must *pray this revival down.* He went back to those woods for prayer three distinct times that morning before he felt ready for the opening service. He found the schoolhouse packed to the doors.

Speaking from John 3:16, he said, "You seem to howl blasphemy about the streets like hell-hounds." The people, knowing this was true, quailed before his words. There were scarcely any dry eyes in the congregation, and the key-keeper finally arose and promised in the afternoon to open the meeting house.

Everybody, he affirms, was at that afternoon service. "The Lord let me loose upon them in a wonderful manner. My preaching seemed to them to be something new. Indeed it seemed . . . that I could rain hail and love upon them . . . that I could rain upon them hail, in love." Great conviction fell upon the place and before the revival ended the spiritual success of Evans Mills attended it.

Then he heard of Sodom, a near-by village, where the inhabitants were filled with wickedness and the only good man in the town was called Lot. He went there for an afternoon service. By a strange coincidence he selected the text, "Up, get you out of this place; for the Lord will destroy the city." Totally ignorant of the circumstances he described ancient Sodom and Lot's part in the long-ago city, and then turned his gospel-guns loose on the congregation.

"The people looked as if they were angry," he relates. "They looked at each other and at me . . . their

anger rose higher and higher as I continued . . . The
congregation began to fall from their seats and cried
for mercy. If I had a sword in each hand, I could not
have cut them off of their seats as fast as they fell. Indeed nearly the whole congregation were either on their
knees or prostrate . . . in less than two minutes . . .
Every one prayed for himself, who was able to speak
at all."

He goes on to say that he was obliged to stop preaching, for no one longer paid attention to his message.
Spiritual cries went up from every corner, and when
Finney left to meet his next appointment that night,
prayers filled his ears with the glad tidings of redemption.

Years later a grandson of the old man, whom they
called Lot, graduated from Oberlin under Finney's instruction, and entered the ministry as his father before
him had done. Both were converted in that Sodom
service.

An elder attended the Antwerp revival who lived about
five miles out of the town in a community of Universal-
ists, who because of their hatred for Finney's Gospel
and the elder's religion would take the wheels off the
elder's carriage so he could not attend the services.
Hence the elder invited Mr. Finney to preach in his
community.

Finney's first sermon swung from the appropriate
text, "Ye serpents, ye generation of vipers, how can ye
escape the damnation of hell?" The convicting Spirit
fell on the congregation, and before the meetings were
finished there was a "complete upturning of the foundations of Universalism. The scene almost equaled that
of Sodom."

Thus to every corner of the surrounding communities the revival spirit penetrated so grandly that Mr. Finney did not even have time to become properly married. After finishing his six-months' term as a home missionary evangelist, he promised the Evans Mills people that he would locate with them for a year.

Having been engaged previously to Miss Lydia Andrews, a young lady of estimable personal character, whose home was in Oneida County, he took leave of his gospel services to marry her in October, 1824. Lydia was one of the youth who prayed for Finney's conversion and took his salvation as a matter of vital and graphic concern. The revivalist says little about the marriage and nothing about the courtship.

"My wife had made preparation," he notes, "for housekeeping; and a day or two after our marriage I left her and returned to Evans Mills to obtain conveyance to transport our goods to that place. I told her that she might expect me back in about a week."

But he had sowed the seeds of a growing revival at Perch River a dozen miles from Evans Mills, and on his way for the conveyance a messenger rushed to him with a request that he speed his steps to the community for a service. The one service broke into a second until the week had passed and still there was no going for his lone wife.

Nor can one blame him too severely, for "the revival spread in the direction of Brownsville, a considerable village several miles." The minister of the city demanded Finney's services, who obedient to the Master's call "spent the winter there, having written to my wife, that such were the circumstances that I must defer coming for her, until God seemed to open the way."

Professor G. Fredrick Wright says of this incident, "It would be doing the keenest injustice to Finney to attribute this long separation from his wife, so soon after their marriage, to any indifference of feeling. It is to be taken purely as an index of the strength of his devotion to the ministerial work to which he felt himself called. For throughout his life he was passionately devoted to his family . . ."

Came spring and the revivalist started for his wife, a hundred miles away, but his horse having loosened a shoe caused him to stop at LeRaysville to have it reset. It was about noon, and the people, knowing who he was, begged him to remain and preach at one o'clock, which he did. The Spirit's glory fell on the audience and Finney, reading God's signs, remained overnight. So great was the interest and the tidal waves of redemption that Finney could not get away, so he sent another man to fetch his waiting wife to him.

This sacrifice, so characteristic of the evangelist, swept a great mass of people into the kingdom, among them the leading judge of the community.

CHAPTER V

PRAYING DOWN REVIVALS

While in prayer God revealed to Finney that he must go to the near-by town of Gouverneur. "Of the place, I knew nothing ," said Mr. Finney, "except that there was much opposition to the revival in Antwerp. I can never tell how or why the Spirit of God made that revelation to me. But I knew then, and I have no doubt now, that it was a direct revelation from God to me . . . But in prayer the thing was all shown to me, as clear as light . . . that God would pour out his Spirit there."

This is characteristic of Mr. Finney's contacts with spiritual illuminations. He learned to wait on God until the divine plan unfolded to his thinking and then he acted speedily. Shortly he saw a man from Gouverneur and told him of the revelation, asking him to pass word to the brethren that he would soon be over and to prepare "for the outpouring of the Lord's Spirit."

This seemed to be a step marked with unwarranted audacity, a faith step this man of God never failed to take when inwardly wrought upon by the Spirit. Religion there was of a low state and the messenger himself "as cold as an iceberg."

In the Spirit's time, when the LeRaysville revival had finished its soul-redeeming work, God said, "Go to Gouverneur; the time has come." First Finney sent his prayer-partner Father Nash ahead to prepare the people for his coming, and on the appointed time, after much prayer by the two workers, "there was a general turning out of the people."

God gave Finney his first text and he went into the pulpit "and let my heart out. The word took powerful effect." This Spirit dependence caused the evangelist never to miss his mark with texts and messages. Before going into the pulpit he made it a practice to bathe his soul in prayer praying away all interferring mental patterns, so the path to his own mind could be directly opened to the whisperings of the Spirit.

The next morning a Universalist doctor challenged Finney to a religious debate. The revivalist accepted on the spot, which was in a tailorshop. Back and forth the arguments went, Finney soon gaining the soul-strangling hold on his opponent until the doctor's friends slipped out of the shop and the man was left alone. Finally the doctor was defeated and went directly home to pace the floor with God's convicting Spirit not only challenging his arguments but his soul's downward career as well.

"His agony became intense," says the evangelist. "He surrendered himself up to his convictions and soon after expressed hope in Christ." In a few days his companions in Universalism, of whom he was the bell sheep, were brought in and the revival made a clean sweep of them all.

In the same town a group of youth banded together to break up the revival, but Father Nash took matters in hand and under God's illumination said, "Now mark me, young men. God will break your ranks in one week, either by converting some of you, or by sending some of you to hell . . ."

Finney was over-wrought as to Nash's seemingly bold prediction and would have spoken to this man of prayer, but shortly the truth of his denunciation was verified by one of the youth accepting Christ, the rest soon to follow.

This man Nash, co-partner in prayer with Finney, proved a valuable asset to the revival, for as in each case he gave himself to prayer, his opponents said, "It is impossible for him to pray in secret, for he can be heard a half-mile off." But pray he did until the heavens opened and rained down glory and revivals. One man heard him praying a great distance off and became so convicted of sin that he early sought God's face for redemptive grace.

When the majority of the Gouverneur people had been converted, Finney went to DeKalb, sixteen miles farther north, where the Methodists sometime before had a revival in which many people fell under divine power. The Presbyterian neighbors made light of this and bad blood existed henceforth between the two groups.

"I had not preached long," says Finney of this revival, "before one evening just at the close of my sermon, I observed a man fall from his seat near the door . . . From what I saw I was satisfied that it was a case of falling under the power of God as the Methodists would express it, and I supposed it was a Methodist . . . But on inquiry I learned that it was one of the principal members of the Presbyterian church . . ."

The remarkable thing was that during this revival there were several cases of the Presbyterians falling under the power, but none among the Methodists. This of course healed the wound between the two groups and knit them together into a fighting unit for God's battle under Finney's leadership.

A Roman Catholic who came from Ogdensburg to measure the preacher for a suit of clothes was converted on the spot and this spread the revival in all directions. Finney had no chance nor occasion to preach, for everywhere people were seeking the Lord. Several people came from the tailor's town to be converted and on returning home they scattered this holy fire.

"Finney could only sit still," says A. M. Hills, "and see the salvation of the Lord, by the spontaneous movement of the Holy Ghost in convicting and converting sinners."

In October, 1825, Finney with his wife attended the Synod at Utica, where a wide door was open to his ministry. But before he left for the Synod a marvelous experience came to him. His words can best tell it:

"Unless I had the experience of prayer I could do nothing. If even for a day or an hour I lost the spirit of grace and supplication, I found myself unable to preach with power and efficiency, or to win souls by personal conversation. For several weeks before going to the Synod I was very strongly exercised in prayer and had an experience somewhat new to me.

"I found myself so much exercised and so borne down with the weight of immortal souls, that I was constrained to pray without ceasing. Some of my experiences indeed alarmed me. A spirit of importunity sometimes came upon me so that I would pray to God that He had made a promise to answer prayer and I could not and would not be denied. I felt so certain that He would hear me that frequently I found myself saying to Him:

" 'I hope Thou dost not think that I can be denied. I come with Thy faithful promises in my hand, and I can not be denied.' My impression was that the answer was very near, even at the door; and I felt myself strengthened in the Divine life, put on the harness for a mighty conflict with the powers of darkness and expected soon to see a far more powerful outpouring of the Spirit of God."

Nor did God disappoint this praying disciple, for larger spheres of spiritual usefulness were soon to open.

At the Synod Finney met Mr. Gale, then in broken health, who asked him to visit his country home near Western where he was living, and where the Presbyterian church was pastorless. Finney got there in time for the midweek prayer meeting when the elders threw long and barren prayers at God. This stirred Finney's heart and he says, "God inspired me to give them a terrible searching . . . They all wept, confessed and broke their hearts before God."

He was begged to remain over Sunday, and on Friday his mind was greatly aroused by the Spirit; consequently he prayed the day through. On Sunday the house was packed and "God came down with power upon the people," who realized a revival was to bless them. The evangelist arranged to preach in different parts of the town, and the startling experiences of former revivals were repeated.

These meetings spread their tidings to Rome, where Moses Gillett was pastor. Hearing Finney at Western, Gillett said, "Brother Finney, it seems to me that I have a new Bible. I never understood the promises as I now do." This led the evangelist to see God was preparing for a mighty stir in Rome. He sent the pastor back to lay its foundation by appointing an inquiry meeting at which the Spirit fell in great power.

Finney said of the Rome meeting, "It would not be possible for one who had never witnessed such a scene to realize what the force of the truth sometimes is under the power of the Holy Spirit. It was indeed a two-edged sword." The state of things was extraordinary as people began to call in every direction for Finney and the pastor to pray for them. Strong men were Spirit-struck as though they were babes. Meetings lasted till midnight and the courthouse, where the services were held, was crowded time and time again each day. Ministers rushed from the neighboring towns and were filled with awe and moved with amazement at what they saw.

They had dreamed of such flood tides of revival glory sweeping their land and now to see them lifted high their hope in God. Nearly all professional and prominent people in the city embraced religion. One opposer was struck dead during the time. Gillett's whole congregation was converted, and it was reported that in twenty days five hundred were brought into the kingdom in Rome.

The story raced to Utica, where excitement over the soul-altering results ran high. Said a leading citizen of Utica, a banker, when he first heard Finney, "That man is mad, and I should not be surprised if he set the town on fire." He refused to attend the meetings, but affirmed later to the directors of the bank, "Say what you will, there is something very remarkable in the state of things at Rome. Certainly no human power or eloquence has produced what we see there . . . There is no accounting for that state of feeling by any philosophy, unless there is something divine in it." Shortly he was converted.

These Rome stories produced a spirit of prayer at Utica, where people prayed for days on end. During a funeral conducted by Samuel Aiken, pastor of the Presbyterian Church at Utica, the revival spirit broke out, so Finney moved the base of operations from Rome to Utica. Within a short while five hundred more converts were reported and the leading hotel in the city became a center of revival power, where transients, as they stopped there, would be converted before going on their way.

Said Dr. Aiken, "The probable number of converts in Utica is about five hundred . . . More than a hundred have united with the First Presbyterian Church; numbers with the Methodists and Baptists . . . Some few individuals have differed from their brethren with regards to the propriety of some measures; but . . . none so hardened in unbelief as not to adore and rejoice in it."

Came a proud school teacher from a near-by town to see for herself the results of Finney's revivals. Spurred by curiosity she was soon lingering to pray, and after her majestic conversion she married a Mr. Gulick, later to become a missionary to the Sandwich Islands, where together they did great work for Christ.

Among the Utica converts was Theodore Weld who afterwards became notable in anti-slavery circles. He was then a student at Hamilton and on hearing Finney denounced his work as fanaticism and boasting. Finney quietly spoke a few words to the youth about his redemption and then left him to his conscience. That night Weld paced the floor in the throes of soul upheaval, only to quiet the spiritual tempest in confession and submission to Finney's Christ.

During the Utica meeting the Oneida Presbytery convened in the revival city and one minister made a violent denunciatory speech against such evangelistic outbursts. Several of the brethren gave themselves seriously to prayer. Fearing the untoward results of such an attack, they besought the divine Hand to turn the wheels of fate so the speech's effects might be counterbalanced. The next morning the preacher who dared thus challenge the Spirit's word *died in bed*.

One evening Finney preached at New York Mills, a mill community skirting Utica. Here he was asked by his brother-in-law to visit the cotton factory where he was in charge. As Finney entered the mill, he noticed a girl whose fingers were trying to tie a broken thread. She became confused, finally burst into tears.

"When I came within eight or ten feet of her," he says, "I looked solemnly at her. She observed it, and was quite overcome, and sank down and burst into tears. The impression caught almost like powder and in a few moments all in the room were in tears. The feeling spread through the factory. The owner . . . said to the superintendent, 'Stop the mill, and let the people attend to religion; for it is more important that our souls should be saved than that this factory should run.' "

The results? Finney says he never attended a more powerful meeting. "The revival went through the mill with astonishing power and in a few days nearly all were converted." And there were hundreds working in the mill. It was a gracious deluge of Pentecost that swept in upon them as created by the godly and Spirit-led presence of Mr. Finney.

From Rome and Utica during that summer Finney preached in the surrounding communities and a report made by a Presbyterian minister affirms that no less than three thousand conversions occurred during that time. After eight months not one case of apostasy had been reported among the number.

In his Memoirs Finney stops long enough in delineating these remarkable results to give a glimpse of the messages God used. "The doctrines I preached in these revivals were those I always preached," he notes. ". . . we pressed the duty of instant surrender to God. We told them the Spirit was striving with them to induce them now to give Him their hearts, now to believe and to enter at once upon a life of devotion to Christ . . .

"We told them . . . that they were in danger of grieving the Spirit of God away. We insisted on immediate submission as the only thing that God could accept at their hands and that all delay under any pretext whatever was rebellion against God. It became very common under my preaching for persons to be convicted and converted in the course of a few hours and sometimes in the course of a few minutes.

"Such sudden conversions were alarming to many good people and they predicted the converts would fall away . . . But the event proved that among those sudden conversions were some of the most influential Christians that have ever been in that region of the country. This has been my experience through all my ministry."

In the summer of 1826 the Utica revival attracted the attention of Dr. Dirck Lansing, Presbyterian pastor in Auburn and one of the Auburn Seminary founders, who insisted on the revivalist coming to this city, where "he went and preached with great power and marked success."

Attending the revival was a physician, an elder of the church, who was felled to the floor by the Holy Spirit coming upon him. Also a Universalist stirred up contention among the attendants and before long Finney arose, with no premeditation, and was led to speak from the text, "Let us alone." The Universalist was Spiritstruck, fell to the floor and cried in a terrific manner until Christ spoke blessed peace to his war-torn soul.

The church was worldly in attire and conformed to the dress of sinful designs. After one of Finney's sermons Dr. Lansing arose and plead with his people to turn to God. Finney stopped him, saying, "Mr. Lansing, I do not believe such remarks from you can do any good while you wear a ruffled shirt and a gold ring, and your wife and the ladies of your family sit . . . dressed as leaders in the fashions of the day."

Dr. Lansing took the rebuff, threw himself from the pulpit and wept like a child. The people dropped their heads and under the moaning of their sobs the Spirit moved upon them. Public confession by the church was made, as their pastor led them, saying, "If these things are an offence, I will not wear them."

The Troy pastor, Dr. N. S. S. Beman and the session of his Presbyterian church invited Finney to labor with them during the autumn and winter of 1826-27. It was here that opposition to Finney's work finally came to a head. Some of the members thought Finney permitted fanaticism and spiritual wildfire to control his revivals, and really gave birth to movements which were too mobified and emotionally jittery to be allowed a place in Gospel work.

Finney, however, in spite of these tirades, preached on with a divine anointing. These attacks were augmented by the fact that the pastor's wife was a vixen and caused no little confusion among the people. Leading infidels of the city were mowed down like hay before the onslaughts of the Holy Spirit. Self-righteous churchmen were convicted as also were the skeptics of the community.

One of the converts, then a lad of fifteen, said to Finney, "I was completely rolled up in the sermon and it carried me right along . . . I gave my all to Christ." This lad was John T. Avery, later to become a noted evangelist and to win thousands to his Redeemer.

The Troy glory spread to New Lebanon, where in spite of opposition from within the church ranks and from the devil's outward attacks a great spiritual awakening took place. It was here the opposition to Finney's revival measures came to a sudden and sullen head.

Chapter VI

PRAYING THROUGH CLOUDS OF OPPOSITION

CLOUDS of growing opposition to Finney's methods and measures darkened the horizon of his work. For some time these had been appearing and finally the evangelist's soul was so wrought upon by the Spirit that he sought refuge in prayer.

Father Nash in a letter dated May 11, 1826, said, "The work of God moved forward in power in some places against dreadful opposition. Mr. Finney and I have been burned in effigy. We have frequently been disturbed in our religious meetings. Sometimes the opposers make a noise in the house of God . . . There is almost as much writing, intrigue, lying and reporting of lies as there would be if we were on the eve of a presidential election . . . But I think the work will go on."

False statements were sent to the press by his enemies. His meetings were alleged to be boisterous and to run to unreasonable hours. His prayers were said to irreverent and his pulpit language harsh, and women to be permitted to pray in mixed gatherings. Finney was accused of adopting such means as the inquiry room, the anxious seat, and handbills to forward his work.

While these clouds were blackening his sky, Finney felt a divine urge to pray them away. He said nothing publicly or privately about the accusations, merely looked to God for direction and guidance.

"I looked to God with great earnestness day after day to be directed," says the revivalist, "asking Him to show me the path of duty and to give me grace to out-ride the storm . . . The Lord showed me as in a vision what was before me. He drew so near to me while I was engaged in prayer that my flesh literally trembled on my bones. I shook from head to foot under the full sense of the presence of God.

"At first and for some time it seemed more like being on top of Sinai amidst its full thundering than in the presence of the cross of Christ. Never in my life was I so awed and humbled before God as then . . .

"After a season of great humiliation before Him there came a great lifting up. God assured me that He would be with me and uphold me; that no opposition should prevail against me; that I had nothing to do in regard to this matter but to keep about my work and wait for the salvation of God.

"The sense of God's presence and all that passed between my soul and God at that time I can never describe. It led me to be perfectly trustful, perfectly kind and to have nothing but the most kindly feelings toward all the brethren that were misled, and were arraying themselves against me. I felt assured that all would come out all right; that my true course was to leave everything to God and to keep about my work; and as the storm gathered and the opposition increased I never for one moment doubted how it would result. I never spent a waking hour in thinking about it, when to all outward appearances it seemed as if all the churches of the land . . . would unite to shut me out of their pulpits."

Only with such assurance was Finney able to go on preaching Christ's freedom to those shackled by sin. These storm clouds grew as he was laboring in Auburn and Troy only to reach their full potency while evangelizing in New Lebanon. And it is odd that of all people ministers should carry the banner of opposition. Such however was the case. Finney in no wise aimed to compete with them in their churches, for his primal desire was to labor where others would not go.

"When Mr. Finney and I began our race, we had no thought of going amongst ministers," writes Father Nash. "Our highest ambition was to go where there was neither minister nor reformation and try to look up the lost sheep, for whom no man cared. We began and the Lord prospered . . . But we go into no man's parish unless called . . . We have room enough to work and work enough to do."

William R. Weeks, a pastor at Paris Hill, began the opposition on theological lines. Weeks held as Finney asserts that "both sin and holiness were produced in the mind by a direct act of Almighty Power; that God made men sinners or holy at His sovereign discretion . . . that in fact God was the only proper agent in the universe and that all creatures acted only as they were moved and compelled to act by His irresistible power; that every sin in the universe both of men and of devils was the result of a direct irresistible act on the part of God."

Weeks sent out under label of his newly formed Oneida Association letters in which Finney and his friends were said to "call men hard names," "report great, powerful revivals which afterwards came to little or nothing," "use injudicious treatment of young converts," "give heed to impressions," "allow anybody and everyboby to speak and pray in promiscuous meetings."

From Trenton, New York, a Unitarian minister sent forth a pamphlet denouncing Finney's evangelism in tones that neared the brimstone mark. He grossly misrepresented the work. Here is his description of the inquiry meetings: "They are generally, if not always, held in the night. The room is darkened, so that persons can only see to walk and discover each other; and the reign of usual silence is interrupted only now and then by a dolorous groan . . . "

It was not necessary for Finney to answer such silly accusation nor did he intend to do so. But the Oneida Presbytery held on September 8, 1826, appointed a committee to make inquiry and to give forth a statement of the true nature of the revival. It was a bulky answer in some sixty-seven pages of closely printed material, consisting of three parts.

"He possesses," said the answering ministers in speaking of Mr. Finney, chief leader of the meetings, "a discriminating and self-balanced mind; has a good share of courage and decision; possesses naturally a good temper; is frank and magnanimous in his deportment . . . and on the whole is as well calculated to be extensively useful in promoting revivals of religion as any man of whom we have knowledge. To say that he never errs, is more than can with truth be said of any man . . . "

The second part of the Report goes into detail as to the nature of the revivals and affirms that the converts have been numerous, conviction for sins has been deep, backsliding has been less common than usual and a strong spirit of prayer marks the converts, who "have manifested more joy and stronger hope than in any preceding revivals among us . . . "

The third part of the Report discusses the means used to promote the revivals, which briefly were: "Seasons of fasting and prayer . . . confession of sin in churches

. . . church discipline . . . visiting from house to house
. . . preaching the Gospel . . . *with great plainness and
earnestness* . . . union of feeling and effort in churches
has promoted this revival . . . meetings of inquiry have
been blessed . . . urging awakening sinners to immediate
repentance . . . visits of ministers, professors and others
where revivals had commenced have had a powerful
effect in extending the work . . . the preaching of the
evangelists . . . united, agonizing, persevering prayer
. . . the instruction given in Sabbath schools and Bible
classes has been eminently blessed."

This Report put caution in the heart of local opposition, but it did not satisfy some of the nosy brethren
over New England way, who decided to send a delegation
to New Lebanon to see for themselves as to the nature of
the irregularities marking the revival. So Asahel
Nettleton and Lyman Beecher crossed the hills into
New York to straighten out the Gospel kinks which were
reported to be tying knots in the evangelism of the back-
woods preacher.

Nettleton himself was the most popular evangelist of
New England at that time and up until then had won
many souls to Christ. Many thought his evangelistic pro-
cedures were innovations from the old Gospel line, nevertheless he wanted to bring the light to this new revivalist.
Nettleton, when the discussions began, was forty-four,
nine years older than Finney.

Lyman Beecher was then the most popular pastor of
Boston and its leading pastoral evangelist. Nettleton
was accused by Dr. E. N. Kirk as not being quite fair,
"For I am informed that no revivalist or evangelist in
our day has so abounded in new measures, contrivances
and management as he." But at the time he was broken

in health and the rising star from the woods of New York might have tinged him with jealousy.

Be that as it may, a careful check of his biography shows only four hundred converts in the next ten years. "He never recovered himself," affirms A. M. Hills.

And Beecher's star as president of Lane Seminary years later was eclipsed when the students said, "At Lane we study Finney more than we do Beecher."

July 18, 1827, the New Lebanon convention was duly called and many important names were among the ministers who were to sit in judgment on Finney's work, names that to us now mean but little, which then however carried great weight in religious circles.

Nettleton and Beecher came fully persuaded against revivals of Finney's type. Beecher was somewhat testy when asked certain questions about his beliefs, answering, "We have not come here to be catechised and our spiritual dignity forbids us to answer any such questions." And the two Bostonians even tried to keep Finney and his associates from testifying in their behalf, but the moderator and the rest of the convening ministers would have no such shameful action on their minutes. So they gladly heard the side of those who believed in the revival.

It was quite a tempest while it was going on. The longer the evidence poured in sustaining Finney's revival conduct the more nervous and agitated became Nettleton. He recognized he and Beecher were losing ground and outside of the disgruntled minister Weeks, the crowd was for Finney and his soul saving efforts.

The first resolution adopted affirmed a hope that greater revivals were to be expected, and through to the end the evangelistic note prevailed and Finney was vindicated.

In Nettleton's Memoirs he mentions specifically some of Finney's measures he objected to, such as, "praying for persons by name; encouraging females to pray and exhort in promiscuous assemblies; calling upon persons to come to the anxious seat; or to rise up in the public assembly to signify that they had given their hearts to God or had made up their mind to attend to religion."

Such contentions seem unworthy of great men viewed in the light of today. They were however means of testing Finney's soul-fiber, and instead of discouraging, they actually drove him to a nearer shelter under the Almighty's wings. Throughout the time Finney was possessed of a quiet mental attitude and none of the railings brought disturbance to his holy rest in God.

"I have labored extensively in this country and in Great Britain," Finney wrote years later, "and no exceptions have been taken to my measures . . . I have always and everywhere used all the measures I used in those revivals . . . Were I to live my life over again, I think that with the experience of more than forty years in revival labors I should under the same circumstances use substantially the same measures that I did then."

In all this he was humble and gave honor to God for his success. "It was no wisdom of my own that directed me," he affirms. "I was made to feel my ignorance and dependence and led to look continually to God for His guidance. I had no doubt then, nor have I ever had, that God led me by His Spirit to take the course I did . . . I never did or could doubt that I was divinely directed.

"I bless the Lord that I was kept from being diverted from my work by their opposition and that I never gave myself any uneasiness about it . . . God had given me the assurance that He would overrule all opposition . . . Under this divine assurance I went forward with a single eye and a trustful spirit."

When Beecher returned to his Boston pulpit, he remarked about his trip into the woods, "We crossed the mountains expecting to meet a company of boys, but we found them to be full-grown men."

The subject of these discussions came up at the Presbyterian General Assembly, held the following May, 1828, in Philadelphia, and a truce was signed which wiped from the slate all further publication of pamphlets and pro and con discussions on the subject. Beecher as well as Finney signed it, though Finney says he has no recollection of signing such a paper. However his signature is unquestionably upon it.

This convention, thought to put Finney upon the ecclesiastical chopping block, merely served to spread his fame to broader and more important fields of service. It gave him a wide open door to the nation's leading cities.

In Beecher's biography he is reported as saying to the evangelist, "Finney, I know your plan, and you know I do; you mean to come to Connecticut, and carry a streak of fire to Boston. But if you attempt it, as the Lord liveth, I'll meet you at the state line and call out the artillerymen and fight every inch of the way to Boston and then I'll fight you there."

This is a brave threat, proving the greatest may err, for in a short time Finney was in Boston preaching in Beecher's church! And while preaching there Beecher told Finney, that he "had never seen a man with whose theological views he so entirely accorded as he did with mine." Beecher even assisted with the inquiry room meetings in the basement of his church.

Chapter VII

HIS ENLARGED EVANGELISTIC FIELD

THE New Lebanon Convention was God's means of enlarging Finney's field of evangelism. He had labored around in one section of New York until then, but God had yet other spheres where his revivals must sweep. Revival truth persecuted as it had been was to spring forth with a renewed vigor.

During the convention a young lady from Stephentown attended Finney's meetings, and being greatly attracted by their results she insisted that the evangelist come to her home church. This was an endowed church, the only one in the town, which due to a lack of pastoral interest had run down and the minister "finally became an open infidel."

Finney promised to go, provided the girl had a gentle horse. The girl laughed at this, but Finney replied, "If the Lord wants me to go to Stephentown the devil will prevent it if he can." Suffice it to remark the horse ran away twice on the trip and came near killing ˙hem.

After the first service Finney said he could hear the girl, Maria by name, praying nearly all night for God's blessings. A spirit of prayer came upon the evangelist and soon God's sword was being wielded with mighty success. God struck down the infidel preacher and during the meeting he died a horrible death. Large families, one with sixteen and another with seventeen children, were converted.

"The spirit of prayer," says the evangelist, "had come powerfully upon me . . . the praying power so manifestly spreading and increasing, the work soon took on a very powerful type; so much so that the word of the Lord would cut the strongest men down and render them helpless."

Zebulon Shipherd, a celebrated lawyer, heard of the revival as he was attending court in Albany and decided to visit it. Out of this came a fellowship which finally took Finney to the teacher's chair in Oberlin, for J. J., Zebulon's son, founded Oberlin and invited Finney to head its school of theology.

Before the revival was completed nearly all the town had been converted. "The striking characteristics of this revival," Finney affirms, "were a mighty spirit of prevailing prayer; overwhelming conviction . . . sudden and powerful conversions . . . great love and abounding joy of the converts . . . This revival occurred . . . immediately after the (New Lebanon) convention. The opposition had received its deathblow."

In these services was a Rev. Mr. Gilbert, pastor of a Wilmington, Delaware, Presbyterian church, who was visiting his father. Seeing God's mighty hand displayed in salvation, the minister invited Finney to hold a meeting for him, though he himself did not believe in revivals (till then) for he felt that evangelism took the work of soul saving out of God's hands, "that God would convert sinners in His own time."

Before the Spirit could move, Finney knew the minister's views on redemption must be altered, so each day the revivalist talked long and seriously with the pastor. For two hours one Sunday Finney threw out the truth of man's ability to decide for salvation and the congregation drank it in while the preacher "brought out strongly the contrast between my views and the views in which they had been instructed, some laughed, some wept, some were manifestly angry."

The poor preacher squirmed and when the meeting was dismissed, a lady whispered in his ears, "Mr. Gilbert, what do you think of that?" "It is worth five hundred dollars," he replied, adding that until then he had "never preached the Gospel."

God was now ready for Finney to spread his evangelistic glory in a large city and through James Patterson, a Presbyterian pastor in Philadelphia, this was to take place. Patterson invited Finney to preach in his church prophesying, "If the Presbyterian ministers in this city find out your views, and what you are preaching to the people, they will hunt you out of the city as they would a wolf."

Said Finney, "I cannot help it. I can preach no other doctrine; and if they must drive me out of the city, let them do it, and take the responsibility. But I do not believe that they can get me out."

Finney had heard from God and knew he was right. The glory broke in upon this Brotherly Love city and from church to church Finney went, preaching there for nearly eighteen months until the winter of 1828-29. One sermon, "There Is One Mediator Between God and Man," he repeated by request nightly for seven nights in seven different churches.

Finally Finney located in the Race Street German Church, seating three thousand and central to the entire city, and there preached steadily for many months. About midsummer of 1829, he visited his wife's folk in Oneida county and on returning to Philadelphia where he labored till midwinter, he said, "In all this time there was no abatement of the revival . . . The converts became numerous in every part of the city."

Then came the lumbermen's revival, doubtless unequalled in all literature of evangelism. Finney's words best tells it thus:

"In the spring of 1829, when the Delaware was high, the lumbermen came down with their rafts . . . At that time there was a large tract . . . called by many the 'lumber region,' that extended toward the headwaters of the Delaware. Many persons were engaged in getting out lumber there . . . Many of the lumbermen were raising families in that region . . . They had no schools, and at that time had no churches or religious privileges.

"These men that came down with lumber attended our meetings and quite a number of them were hopefully converted. They went back into the wilderness and began to pray for the outpouring of the Holy Spirit, and to tell the people around them what they had seen in Philadelphia and to exhort them to attend to their salvation.

"Their efforts were immediately blessed and the revival began to take hold and to spread . . . It went on in a most powerful and remarkable manner. It spread to such an extent that in many cases persons would be convicted and converted who had not attended any meetings and who were almost as ignorant as heathen.

"Men who were getting out lumber and were living in little shanties alone, or where two or three or more were together, would be seized with such conviction that it would lead them to wander off and inquire what they should do, and they would be converted, and thus the revival spread.

"In the spring of 1831 two or three men from this lumber region came to see me and to inquire how they could get some ministers to go in there. They said that not less than five thousand people had been converted . . . that the revival had extended itself along for eighty miles and there was not a single minister of the gospel there.

"I have never been in that region but from all I have ever heard about it I have regarded that as one of the most remarkable revivals that have occurred in this country. The spark that was struck into the hearts of those few lumbermen that came to Philadelphia spread over that forest and resulted in the salvation of a multitude of souls."

During the winter of 1828-29 Finney held a short meeting in Reading, Pennsylvania, where the minister died suddenly during the revival, which caused a great seriousness to settle upon the people. This was followed by a brief series of services at Lancaster where many were brought into the kingdom through a group of prayer meetings.

During this Lancaster revival one night Finney had the audience arise and make immediate decision for Christ. Two men near the door remained seated, and as they left the building they discussed the matter of the evangelist's appeal. One of the men, evidently moved upon greatly by the Spirit, started home through the dark and on his way he fell over the curbstone and broke his neck . . . "called, but lost!"

In the summer of 1829 Mr. Finney was urged to hold meetings in Columbia, New York, where there was a large German Church, "only about ten of whom knew what it was to have a change of heart." Finney gave himself to much prayer and the Lord moved mightily upon the people. "That revival," says the evangelist, "continued to spread until it reached and converted nearly all the inhabitants of the town."

From this community a colony settled at Galesburg, Illinois, where Mr. Gale, Finney's teacher and pastor at Adams, had founded a town and also Knox College.

During the summer while Finney was on a visit to his wife's parents, Anson G. Phelps, the philanthropist, learning that Finney had not been invited to hold revivals in New York City due to the controversy which Nettleton and Beecher had stirred up, rented a vacant church in Vandewater Street, "and sent an urgent request for me to come there and preach."

Shortly a Universalist church was offered for sale and it was purchased and fitted for Mr. Finney's use. Here he laid siege to the city in a fifteen-months' revival. While in New York City Finney met Arthur Tappan and through him a brother Lewis, who at the time was a Unitarian. Finney's influence upon Lewis and the prayers of his brother caused him to turn from his former agnostic views and serve Christ. To the end of his life he remained a faithful friend of the evangelist. When Oberlin College was formed a few years later Arthur Tappan was very liberal in his gifts toward the young institution.

Out of the New York revival came the establishment of the Free Presbyterian Church called free because there were no pew rents, a movement which soon spread rapidy throughout the city.

In the summer of 1830 Finney was invited to hold a meeting in the Third Presbyterian Church of Rochester, which at the time was without a pastor. On investigation he discovered the outlook to be dark indeed, for there was dissention among the Presbyterian churches of the city as well as little spiritual life in evidence. Wickedness abounded, dance halls flourished and a low moral tone marked the city. After much prayer Finney says, "My mind became entirely decided . . . that Rochester was the place to which the Lord would have me go."

Soon the Christians of the city united. One of his first converts was the wife of a prominent lawyer, who previously had been a very worldly woman and "did not want a revival which would greatly interfere with the pleasures and amusements that she had promised herself that winter." Her remarkable conversion caused no little excitement in the city and was the means of spreading the revival's influence.

"I had never," says Mr. Finney, "except in rare instances, until I went to Rochester used as a means of promoting revivals what has since been called 'the anxious seat'. I had sometimes asked persons in congregations to stand up . . . From my own experience and observation I found that with the higher classes especially the greatest obstacle to be overcome was their fear of being known as anxious inquirers . . .

"I had found also that something was needed to make the impression on them that they were expected at once to give up their hearts . . . something that would commit them publicly to the service of Christ . . . At Rochester I first introduced this measure."

A few days after the conversion of the lawyer's wife he gave his call for all who were willing to renounce their sins and give themselves to God to come forward to certain seats which had been vacated and offer themselves to God, while he made them a subject of prayer. A great number responded.

"It was soon seen," he affirms, "that the Lord was aiming at the highest classes of society. The lawyers, physicians, merchants and indeed all the most intelligent people became interested and more easily influenced . . . A large number of the lawyers, nearly all the judges, bankers, merchants and master mechanics and leading men and women in the city were converted."

The spirit of prayer was poured out "so powerfully that some people staid away from public services to pray, being unable to restrain their feelings under preaching." An Abel Clary could not go to the meetings and he prayed nearly all the time night and day, and in such an agony of mind that he seemed possessed of an unbearable soul burden.

Said a man with whom Clary lived, "Sometimes he cannot stand on his knees, but will lie prostrate on the floor, and groan and pray." Father Nash along with three deacons were affected in such a manner.

Practically everyone in the city was converted. "The only theater in the city," says Finney, "was converted into a livery stable and the only circus into a soap and candle factory . . . the grog shops were closed."

Ten thousand were said to be converted during the meeting. Finney's mighty preaching and all this prevailing prayer were blessed of God in a marvelous way. Ministers and prominent people from neighboring towns, cities and even neighboring states came to be under the influence of such revival fire. On returning home they too had their part in spreading this evangelistic glory.

Said Beecher, once the opponent of Finney's revivals, now the praiser, "That was the greatest work of God and the greatest revival of religion that the world has ever seen in so short a time. One hundred thousand were reported as having connected themselves with churches as the results of that great revival. This is unparalleled in the history of the Church and of the progress of religion. In no year during the Christian era have we any account of so great a revival of religion."

Finney addressed the students of the public schools where many of them were converted and a careful check later showed forty became ministers.

Finney said that the key which unlocked the heavens in this revival was the prayer of Clary, Father Nash and the other unnamed folk who laid themselves prostrate before God's throne and besought Him for a divine outpouring.

Feeling wornout after this strenuous campaign, he aimed to rest, but Dr. Nott, president of Union College at Schenectady, invited Finney to labor with his students. The roads were so bad that the evangelist stopped at Auburn to recuperate. Here a few years previous he faced great opposition, but now a petition was signed by many leading people asking him to speak to them on salvation themes. Finney consented to preach on Sundays only, so that he might regain his strength during the weeks.

Before the meeting was over every signer of the petition was converted along with about five hundred other people. One of the first men to land at the anxious seat was the leader of the opposition five years previous.

Toward the close of this meeting a messenger came inviting the revivalist to Buffalo, which invitation Finney thought providential and accepted to remain there a month. From here he went to Providence for a "protracted meeting" as they called it. This meeting lasted three weeks. "The Lord poured out His Spirit immediately upon the people, and the work of grace commenced immediately," he relates.

This seemed to be God's roundabout way of getting the evangelist to Boston, from which city the Congregational ministers sent Dr. Wisner, pastor of the Old South Church "to spy out the land." When the invitation was issued to come to Boston in the fall of 1831, Finney held off at first, remembering Beecher's bitterness. However, Catherine Beecher spoke to her father and he in turn issued the invitation himself that finally brought the evangelist to the city.

Finney went first to Edward Beecher's church, Lyman's son and Henry Ward Beecher's brother, where "he preached to a crowded house the most impressive and powerful sermon I ever heard . . . No one can form any conception of the power of his appeal. It rings in my ears even to this day," said Edward Beecher.

"This confirms," writes A. M. Hills. who himself had trained hundreds of preachers during his life, and who had been a student of Finney, "my judgment of Finney's preaching that for matchless power to sway men for good he was easily the greatest preacher . . . of the century."

During the Boston revival Finney was invited to preach three days at Andover, which happened at the time of the Andover Seminary commencement. Forty-two orations were slated to be delivered by the graduating theologues, most of which were never made because of Finney's revival attractions.

"Such was the fame of Mr. Finney," writes Professor Park then teaching at Andover, "that we were compelled to give up our exercises. Only thirty people gathered to hear the discourse of Dr. Justin Edwards (New England's most famous preacher at the time) and they were adjourned."

In Finney's audience, however, there were between two and three hundred preachers and students for the ministry. His sermon was just one hundred minutes long. "It was too earnest to be called theatrical, but in the best sense of the word, it was dramatic. Some of his rhetorical utterances are indescribable."

CHAPTER VIII

NEW YORK CITY'S EVANGELISTIC CENTER

Finney had circled with his revivals the heart of the Eastern part of the nation, and now God was ready for him to move into its very center. For ten years he had been in evangelism. "I had become fatigued, as I had labored about ten years," he says, "as an evangelist without anything more than a few days or weeks of rest during the whole period."

The free church movement had spread in the city from his previous revival and a few of the brethren suggested that they rent the Chatham Street Theater, fit it as a church and Finney come as their pastor. Lewis and Arthur Tappan in the summer of 1832 thought it would give Finney a chance to recuperate his strength and furnish a settled home for the Finney family, consisting at this time of three children.

"On praying and looking the matter over," says the revivalist, "I decided I would accept the call."

The old theater had been a place of wickedness and when the two men approached the leasee and asked if he would sell his lease, he asked, "What for?" "A church." "You mean to make a church here!" When assured that they did, he burst into tears and said, "You may have it and I will contribute a thousand dollars toward it."

At the close of the morning rehearsal the hymn, "The Voice of Free Grace," was sung after which Arthur Tappan announced to the actors that a pulpit would be placed on the stage when the scenery was removed and that on the following Sunday church would be held in the theater.

The next morning the services where launched by a five-thirty o'clock prayer meeting at which eight hundred persons were present.

More than seven thousand dollars were spent in making the theater into a church auditorium with lecture and Sunday School rooms adjoining. The following Sunday morning, May 6, 1832, Finney preached from the text, "Who is on the Lord's side?" That afternoon the Communion was administered and by the time of the evening service the building was filled to overflowing, many being turned away.

Finney's text was "I call heaven and earth to record against you, that I have set before you life and death, blessing and cursing; therefore choose life, that both thou and thy seed may live." Despite the fact that cholera raged in the city Finney preached for seventy successive evenings to audiences ranging from 1500 to 2500 people.

In addition to preaching services at the Chatham Street Chapel, as it was called after the dedicatory sermon, there were Bible classes, prayer meetings, the circulation of Bibles and religious literature, etc. The workers visited shops, stores, saloons and offices and invited people to attend the meetings. The barroom was turned into a prayer room. The first man to pray in it was an actor, who said, "O Lord, forgive my sins! The last time I was here Thou knowest that I was a wicked actor on this stage. O Lord have mercy on me!"

"When I first went to Chatham Street Chapel I informed the brethren that I did not wish to fill up the house with Christians from other churches as my object was to gather from the world. I wanted to secure the conversions of the ungodly, to the utmost possible extent . . . Conversions were multiplied so much that our church would soon become so large that we would send off a colony; and when I left New York I think we had seven free churches, whose members were laboring . . . to secure the salvation of souls."

Finney's desire in taking this New York church was to show that evangelism at its heights was possible even in a stated pastorate. God's blessings were upon the people from the beginning and Finney won as many souls here as elsewhere. He had a unique method of seating his Christians throughout the three tiers of galleries, of which he says:

"I instructed my church members to scatter themselves over the whole house and to keep their eyes open in regard to any that were seriously affected under the preaching, and if possible to detain them after preaching for . . . prayer. They were true to their teaching and were on the lookout at every meeting . . . they had faith enough to dismiss their fears and to speak to any whom they saw to be affected by the Word. In this way the conversion of a great many souls was secured. They would invite them into those rooms (a room being off of each tier of galleries) and there we would converse and pray with them and thus gather up the results in every sermon."

During the cholera epidemic, which laid Finney low, this church was a great blessing to the sick and the dying. When he finally succumbed to it, the remedy used to cure him proved so disastrous in its results that he was unable to carry on his heavy duties until the following spring of 1833.

Again the Spirit was immediately poured out and there were five hundred known conversions.

"The church," he says, "was a praying, working people. They were thoroughly united, were trained in regard to labors for the conversion of sinners, and were a most devoted and efficient Church of Christ. They would go out into the highways and hedges and bring people to hear preaching, whenever they were called upon to do so. Both men and women would undertake this work. Our ladies were not afraid to go and gather in all classes."

The work of his *free churches*, springing from the Chapel, helped spread his message and revival fires throughout the entire city. "A more harmonious," he says of them, "prayerful and efficient people I never knew than were the members of those *free Churches*."

Finney, having been duly installed as a Presbyterian pastor by the Presbytery, found difficulty as his work grew of administering it along Presbyterian lines, so some of the brethren decided to build a church for him, and persuaded him to sever his denominational lines and become a Congregationalist.

From the beginning of his evangelism, and even of his converted life, he had not been in harmony with the hyper-dogmatic positions taken by his denominational brethren. He could never feel that the atonement of Christ was limited in extent but the message of salvation was for everybody. The two churches where he first evangelized saw this battle well fought.

"So far as his theological views were concerned," writes Beardsley, "they probably were no more welcome in Congregational circles than they had been among the Presbyterians, and it is doubtful whether his taking

up with the Congregational form of church government
was regarded as an asset to that denomination, for
theologically, during practically the whole of his life, he
was looked upon with suspicion by the Congregationalists."

In building the Broadway Tabernacle, scene of his
subsequent labors in the city, Finney did the designing
himself. He had been confronted with so many ill-con-
structed auditoriums that he decided to make this to suit
his own mind.

"The plan of the interior of that house was my own,"
he affirms. ". . . An architect was consulted, and I gave
him my plan. But he objected to it, that it would not
appear well, and feared that it would injure his reputation to build a church with such an interior as that."

The building was one hundred feet square, for the
revivalist cared more for acoustics than aesthetics. The
walls were plain brick and set back fifty feet from
Broadway in the center of a built-up block, so no expense should be brought upon them for outside adorn-
ment. The cost of the building was sixty-five thousand
and five hundred dollars. The seating capacity of the
auditorium was twenty-five hundred with arrangements
to take care of another fifteen hundred in emergencies.

The seats were circular around a large square platform about a fourth of the distance from the rear wall.
A deep gallery ran around the walls, save above the
platform. In this manner the entire audience was seated
near the preacher, no listener being more than eighty
feet from the speaker.

This made it possible for Finney to speak with ease
and for the people to hear without difficulty. Under
the choir loft was his study and a large lecture room

which was to have been used to give instructions to the young men preparing for the ministry.

It was found early in Finney's ministry that the *New York Observer*, the Presbyterian religious weekly of New York City, was favorable to Nettleton's views concerning the revivalist, and would print only articles on his side. The friends of Finney and his revival movement decided something ought to be done about the situation. So with Judge Jonas Platt of the Supreme Court and others, a rival paper was projected, called the *New York Evangelist*. Rev. Joshua Leavitt at length was called to edit it. Under the influence of Finney the paper soon had a wide circulation.

In January, 1834, Finney's health failed again which necessitated taking a voyage to the Mediterranean. The weather proved stormy, the quarters close, and the captain was given to drink. At one time when the captain was drunk Finney was forced to navigate the vessel, an ability early acquired on Lake Ontario. The trip required six months and when time came for the evangelist's return he became perturbed in his soul over the status of revivals in the world.

"I feared," he wrote, "that they would decline throughout the country . . . that the opposition that had been made to them had grieved the Holy Spirit. My own health, it appeared to me, had nearly or quite broken down, and I knew of no other evangelist that would take the field and aid pastors in revival work . . . I spent the entire day in prayer in my stateroom or walking the deck in intense agony . . .

"I sought the Lord to go on with His work, and to provide Himself with such instrumentalities as were necessary . . . After a day of unspeakable wrestling and

agony of soul, just at midnight the subject cleared up to
my mind. The Spirit led me to believe that all would
come out all right . . . that I might be at rest . . . that
the Lord would go forward with His work, and give
me strength to take any part in it He desired. But I
had not the least idea what course His providence would
take."

In all of this the design of God was being patterned.
For his soul wrestling came in the early part of July,
and on landing at New York he discovered his friends
had held an anti-slavery meeting on July Fourth where
feeling tided high. Some wretch set fire to the Tabernacle
and burned the roof off. The firemen were so wrought
up that they refused to put the fire out.

Meanwhile Mr. Leavitt had not been as wise as he
should have with the *Evangelist* with reference to the
slavery movement, and the subscriptions were falling
off at the rate of more than fifty a day. He greeted
Finney with the words, "I have ruined the *Evangelist*.
Unless you can do something to restore the *Evangelist*
it will only run till January."

Finney's health caused him to despair, but he promised to take the matter up at the heavenly throne as he
had done on the voyage. God gave him a plan which
was to multiply his usefulness many hundred fold. He
decided to deliver a series of lectures on revivals, which
Leavitt would report in his paper. The following week
Leavitt announced the forthcoming series in the paper
and the subscriptions began to pour in immediately.

"These lectures," Finney relates in his Memoirs,
"were afterward published in a book and called
'Finney's Lectures on Revivals.' Twelve thousand copies
of them were sold as fast as they could be printed;

and here, for the glory of Christ, I would say that they have been reprinted in England and France; they were translated into Welsh and on the Continent were translated into French and German, and were extensively circulated throughout Europe and the colonies of Great Britain.

"They were, I presume, to be found wherever the English language was spoken. After they had been printed in Welsh, the Congregational ministers of the Principality of Wales . . . appointed a committee to inform me of the great revival that had resulted from the translation of those lectures into the Welsh language . . . One publisher in London informed me that his father had published eighty thousand volumes of them.

"These revival lectures, meager as was the report of them, and feeble as they were in themselves, have been instrumental . . . in promoting revivals in England and Scotland and Wales, on the Continent, in Canada, in Nova Scotia, and all over the United States and in the islands of the sea.

". . . I have often been refreshed by meeting with ministers and laymen in great numbers that have been converted . . . through the instrumentality of those lectures . . . When they were first published in the *New York Evangelist* the reading of them resulted in revivals of religion in multitudes of places throughout this country."

Now for more than a century this book has remained the classic on religious revivals. The number of ministers it has instructed on this subject, the souls it has won to the Master, the youth that have been led to the ministry through it and its general influence on kingdom enterprises will never be known until "the books are opened."

Nor did Finney take the glory for the book. He thought it was a divine inspiration. He says, "But this was not of man's wisdom. Let the reader remember that long day of agony and prayer at sea that God would do something to forward the work of revivals . . . I felt certain then that my prayers would be answered, and I have regarded all that I have since been able to accomplish as . . . an answer to the prayers of that day . . .

"He pressed my soul in prayer until I was enabled to prevail and through infinite riches of grace in Christ Jesus I have been many years witnessing the wonderful results of that wrestling with God. In answer to that day's agony He had continued to give me the spirit of prayer."

Back to his Chatham Chapel he went with his ministry until the Broadway Tabernacle was completed; then he moved with his congregation to it. The fall and winter of 1834-35 were greatly blessed with a continuous revival in the Tabernacle.

During this New York pastorate numerous youth who had been converted under Finney's ministry asked their spiritual sire to train them in theology. The revivalist decided to use one of his lecture rooms for this purpose, and despite the lack of physical vigor once characterizing him he determined to deliver a course of theological lectures yearly.

There was a bend in his career, around which Finney could not see, planning that his lectures to theological students should be given elsewhere than at the Broadway Tabernacle.

While Finney in 1833 was building his evangelistic center in New York City over in the woods of Ohio young Rev. John Jay Shipherd was founding a com-

munity devoted solely to religious living and high
moral resolve. A small colony had gathered in the tim-
ber-sheltered region and opened under the leadership
of Asa Mahan what they called the Collegiate Institute.

The town took its name idealistically from an Alsacian
pastor, John Fredrick Oberlin, whose highly evangelical
life and ministry had proved an inspiration to Shipherd
and his colaborer Philo Stewart. The colonists bound
themselves together to support the Institute by self-
denying means for the purpose of extending God's
kingdom.

A high tone of religion rang through those Lorain
county woods from its very start when the school first
opened its doors in December, 1833. The total attendance at that term consisted of twenty-nine men and
fifteen women.

The following year the trustees of Lane Theological
Seminary in Cincinnati had become alarmed over the
growing abolitionist sentiment and forbid students dis-
cussing slavery views. Dr. Lyman Beecher, the president,
manipulated his school unwisely and many students in
a body marched out on him.

Arthur Tappan saw in this a providential move and
suggested that he finance Finney in an endeavor to start
a school of evangelical theology with these recalcitrant
students. "Mr. Tappan proposed to me," says the evangelist, "that if I would go to some point in Ohio, and
take rooms where I could gather those young men and
give them my views in theology and prepare them for
the work of preaching through the West, he would be at
the entire expense of the undertaking."

Later Asa Mahon, president of the new religious
school, came with Tappan to persuade Finney to go to

Oberlin and build a department of theology or practical religious work. The Lane boys agreed they would attend Oberlin provided Finney came as their teacher of theology.

This indeed seemed quite a far-away plan from the one Finney had under consideration for training youth for the Christian ministry in terms of his own evangelistic fervor. There was much to be considered before the move could be made. Finney's congregations were growing, converts were being made weekly, and the work of God was abounding in this evangelistic center. On the other hand Oberlin was untried, in the heart of the wilderness, and as yet merely an experiment.

Then there was the church to consider. Would they be willing to give him up? And if so, who could carry on his work?

Praying over the invitation Finney made two proposals to the Oberlin authorities, which were: "One was that they (the trustees) should never interfere with the internal regulation of the school . . . The other that we should be allowed to receive colored people on the same condition as we did white people."

These conditions were accepted, and shortly the friends in New York aided by the Tappan brothers soon subscribed an endowment for eight professorships.

"I felt difficulty," relates the evangelist, "in giving up that admirable place for preaching the gospel, where such crowds were gathered within the sound of my voice . . . There was a great difficulty in leaving my church in New York. I had never thought of having my labors at Oberlin interfere with my revival labors and preaching. It was therefore agreed between myself and the church that I should spend my winters in New York and my summers at Oberlin; and that the church would be at the expense of my going and coming. When this was arranged I took my family and arrived in Oberlin at the beginning of the summer, 1835."

Thus God solved the problem of Finney's theological lectures and was thus to add another field of Christian service to this evangelist whose one desire was to spread the cause of revivals through the nation.

CHAPTER IX

EVANGELISM THROUGH EDUCATION

There was yet another phase to Finney's evangelistic career which was to be rounded out under the Spirit's guidance. He had been for many years now a successful revivalist, going from city to city winning souls to his Master. Then he had been an evangelistic pastor, keeping a high tide of salvation running in Chatham Chapel and now at Broadway Tabernacle, proving that a soul-winning pastorate is possible and the normal state for a church.

God had made out of him an evangelistic writer, whose book stirred the fires of revivals in the leading countries of the world.

God had yet another reservoir of his character to tap for evangelism. He was to make the classroom a center of revival glory. This is a broad statement, and contradictory according to modern educational standards, yet true nevertheless.

As a revivalist, as a pastor, as a writer God had enabled Finney to win souls. Now as a teacher he was to win them. To Finney this was the norm. If he could not win souls while teaching them, he would have none of teaching. If he could not have revivals in the college, he felt he had failed. But revivals he had and souls he won whatever the term applied to him, whether evangelist or professor of theology as he was to be.

Oberlin offered little but five hundred acres of land out in Ohio, a band of theological students who would not have their mouths muzzled against expressing their sentiments on slavery, and above all a sturdy group of pioneers of high moral worth.

Speaking of the colonists that settled Oberlin, Wright says, "They subscribed a covenant in which the degeneracy of the church was lamented, the importance of building up institutions of Christian learning . . . was emphasized, and dependence upon the counsel of the Lord was acknowledged. They pledged themselves to hold in possession no more property than they could profitably manage as faithful stewards of God . . .

"They expressed it their intention to eat only plain and wholesome food, to renounce bad habits . . . They expressed it as their desire to discard unwholesome fashions of dress . . .

"They also affirmed their determination to maintain a deep tone of personal piety, to provoke each other to love and good works, to live together in all things as brethren and to glorify God in their bodies and spirits . . . The result was the collection at Oberlin of a class of pioneers of very high character."

The buildings were crude, the work barely started when Finney gave his word to become professor of theology, but the letter telling of this decision created a stir and students began to flock to Oberlin so they might sit under this mighty son of evangelism. To be certain the revival aspect of his work would not be slighted, since there was no building large enough to hold the crowds, Finney was told to bring a tent for his preaching.

"After I was engaged to come," he affirms, "the brethren at Oberlin wrote requesting me to bring a large tent to hold meetings in, as there was no room in the place large enough to accommodate the people. I made this request known to some of the brethren, who told me to go and get a tent made and they would furnish the money . . . It was a circular tent, a hundred feet in diameter . . . At the top of the center pole which supported the tent was a streamer upon which was written in very large characters, 'Holiness to the Lord.'

". . . It was used to some extent to hold protracted meetings in the region round about."

Finney had no sooner settled to his teaching task in June, 1835, than a calamity befell the institution. Arthur Tappan had promised Finney, if needs be, the use of his entire income of $100,000 a year to run the school and upon this promise the evangelist had relied. But on December 16 of that first year Tappan's New York City store burned to the ground. He started business again in face of the coming financial crash which struck the country shortly afterward. Two years later, in May, 1837, he suspended business and went into bankruptcy.

This was a blow to the revivalist. But blows to this man of prayer were no new thing, for he knew how to soften them . . . *on his knees.* "It left us not only without funds," Finney says, ". . . but thirty thousand dollars in debt . . . and to the human view it would seem that the college must be a failure."

This was not a mere pinch in circumstances. It meant hard times for the teaching revivalist. "At one time I saw no means of providing for my family through the winter," he says. "Thanksgiving day came, and found us so poor that I had been obliged to sell my traveling trunk, which I had used in my evangelistic labors, to supply the place of a cow that I had lost . . . I went and preached and enjoyed my own preaching as well,

I think, as I ever did. I had a blessed day to my own soul."

Finney found a place of prayer that morning and submitted the matter wholly to God's discretion. By the time the sermon was over and he had gotten home the answer was in hand. "The answer has come, dear," said his wife handing him a letter.

It was from Josiah Chapin of Providence and contained a check for $200. "He intimated that I might expect more from time to time. He continued to send me six hundred dollars a year for several years, and on this I managed to live."

This is the Finney God could use so grandly in soul saving . . . a Finney, after spending fifteen years in prodigious evangelistic labors, winning tens of thousands of souls to Christ, who did not have enough money to *buy a cow without selling a trunk!* This was the depth of his consecration. He had received liberally, but he had given just as joyously in return.

The long vacation at the school was placed in the winter to enable the students to find employment as teachers when such services were in demand. This gave Finney the winter months to return to his New York City pastorate. The trustees had taken the following action when he was appointed:

"Resolved that with the view of the increased influence of Mr. Finney in the church at large, he have liberty to be absent four or five months of each year . . ."

For three years he spent his summers in Oberlin and his winters with the Tabernacle folk in New York City. Each winter was blessed with a revival in the Tabernacle and Oberlin was in the spiritual throes of a continual revival during his stay.

At this strenuous time it was decided to send friends of the college to England, where Finney's *Revival Lectures* had sold so extensively, and ask for contributions toward Finney's new type of work. The English who had taken Finney's book so to heart gladly sent back thirty thousand dollars, which was used to wipe out the Oberlin debt.

The revival element still ran high in his thinking, for he relates, "We had a blessed reviving, whenever I returned there to preach (New York). We also had a revival here continually. Very few students came here then without being converted."

His health began to fail again, and he discovered he would be unable to continue both tasks. Weighing the two fields of evangelism and service . . . the prosperous Tabernacle as his church or the impoverished college room . . . saving souls through preaching alone or saving them through training preachers with the stamp of his evangelism upon them . . . he decided for the latter. He says:

"I therefore took dismission from my church in New York, and the winter months . . . I spent in laboring in various places to promote revivals of religion."

Before closing, however, his New York work, God had a task for him to complete. He had already written his *Revival Lectures* and God put it in his heart to stir up Christians to their more blessed and more deeply consecrated relations to Christ. So Finney gave lectures to Christians while preaching at the Tabernacle which also were published in the *Evangelist*. These later became a book, *Lectures to Professed Christians*, in which he developed his doctrine of "the deeper experience," "the high walk," "perfect love or sanctification," more fully than he had done elsewhere.

This book was to enjoy a marvelous circulation and to spread his fame as a Christian evangelist to broader fields as well as to add laurels to his name as a man to whom God had entrusted the deeper secrets of His kingdom. "Those sermons to Chrstians were very much the result of a searching that was going on in my own mind," he notes. "I mean that the Spirit of God was showing me many things in regard to the question of sanctification that led me to preach those sermons to Christians."

His soul pilgrimage, resulting in the lectures, is interesting to note. He writes of it thus: "I was also led into a state of great dissatisfaction with my own want of stability in faith and love ... I often felt myself weak in the presence of temptation, and needed frequently to hold days of fasting and prayer, and to spend much time in overhauling my own religious life in order to retain that communion with God and that hold upon the Divine truth that would enable me efficiently to labor for the promotion of revivals of religion."

God did not long withhold the needed spiritual touch to this fully consecrated man who for so many years had walked in the light of Bible truth. God freshly anointed him for his teaching ministry as well as for his public ministry. Here is his story of soul uplift and enlargement:

"That last winter in New York God was pleased to visit my soul with a great refreshing. After a season of great searching of heart, He brought me . . . into a large place and gave me much of that Divine sweetness in my soul ... That last winter I had a thorough breaking up; so much so that sometimes for a considerable period, I could not refrain from loud weeping . . . Such seasons were frequent that winter and resulted in the great renewal of my spiritual strength and enlargement of my views in regard to the privileges of Christians and the abundance of the grace of God."

This gave birth to Finney's doctrine of Christian blessedness or sanctification or the "higher life" as Beardsley calls it. "A topic of absorbing interest at this time in Oberlin was the doctrine of the higher life," writes Beardsley. Finney describes this experience as "the consecration of the whole being to God . . . that state of devotedness to God . . . a state not only of entire but of perpetual unending consecration to God." He taught that the experience was to be sought and obtained through faith as a present and permanent possession.

These views later were enlarged in his book on *Sanctification* and also in his *Systematic Theology,* where as he says, "I discussed the subject of entire sanctification more at large."

The influence of the school began to attract attention as its doctrines often invited criticism. Finney's personality drew a cosmopolitan group of students. David Livingstone, while waiting in 1839 to explore Africa and open it to the Gospel forwarded his first salary money to a younger brother in Scotland urging him to take the money and study under Finney. This he did graduating in 1845.

The attendance at the school increased rapidly from a hundred at the beginning of Finney's work to five hundred in 1840 and more than a thousand ten years later. A few years after Finney's death President Garfield delivering an address to the students affirmed that no college in the land had more effectively touched the nerve centers of the national life and thought and ennobled them than did this institution to which Charles Finney devoted so many years of Christian service.

Finney brought the little school into world-wide renown, and before he had stepped down from his lecture chair he had taught twenty thousand students, touching them with the nobility of his evangelism through preaching as well as through formal classroom instruction.

He took leave of the Tabernacle pastorate April 6, 1837, feeling the task was too much for him. But a year earlier when James Shipherd resigned the pastorate of the Oberlin church due to ill health, Finney was asked to take temporary charge of it. This was to entail upon him a long ministry, and make it possible for him to preach each Sunday to the students he taught during the week.

This temporary pastorate became permanent in May, 1837, and continued thus until advanced age forced the evangelist to relinquish this service in 1872, when he was eighty years old. The stated salary for this ministerial work while teaching was first set at four hundred dollars a year, later to be increased.

"It was indeed a capital event for the church, the community, the college," writes Delavan Leonard, Oberlin historian, ". . . when Mr. Finney accepted his call to the pastorate . . . His audience was one of the very largest in the land and composed of the multitude of impressible youth coming and going, who by the thousand and ten thousand were moulded for godliness and eminent Christian service. They without him would have suffered irreparable loss and in like manner without them the outcome of his life would have been far less."

For some years preaching was held in Colonial Hall, completed in the spring of 1836, but shortly this was too small. In the summers and for commencement the Big Tent continued in use, but at length Finney resolved to build a church, which was enclosed, but not completed, in 1842. Its seating capacity was more than two thousand and it furnished a throne for Finney's Christian eloquence. From its pulpit some of his mightiest sermons were preached.

Finney's desire was that the college and the church should be a unit. He never sought to distinguish between them. For to him teaching and salvation work, or instruction and evangelism were handmaidens in the cause of God's kingdom. For this reason his long pastorate ministry paralleled his teaching ministry in Oberlin.

The growth of the church under Finney's ministry was as steady and permanent as that of the college. By 1860 the membership of the church was 1,545, so a second church was organized with a hundred members and began its services in the college chapel.

Nor was the school without its critics. In order to have a medium for disseminating the truths taught at the college they launched *The Oberlin Evangelist* which soon reached a circulation of five thousand. Finney was a regular contributor to this, by which means he kept in touch with the many friends he had made in evangelism and reached a constituency otherwise impossible for him to touch. Almost every issue, through the twenty-four years of its life, contained a sermon either by Finney or Presiden Mahan. During 1845-46 he contributed a series of thirty-two articles on revivals which supplemented his Lectures on the same subject.

Later the *Oberlin Quarterly* made its appearance, "in which we disabused the public in a great measure in regard to what our real views were."

Finney tells a story, to show the outside feeling toward the college and its evangelistic theology, about how he was driving one day when he came upon an elderly lady, whom he asked to ride with him. They had gone some distance when she inquired, "May I ask to whom I am indebted for this ride?" Finney told her.

"This announcement startled her. She made a motion as if she would sit as far from me as she could; and turning and looking earnestly at me, she said, 'From Oberlin! Why our minister said he would just as soon send a son to the state prison as to Oberlin!'"

Finney's motto was "Souls at any price and under all circumstances." And his college teaching made no difference to him. He could not see why they should not expect a revival atmosphere at the college the same as at the Broadway Tabernacle. If the school went long without a special divine breathing upon faculty and students Finney became worried. Tides of such blessings were continually overflowing the institution.

"During these years . . . the Lord was richly blessing us within," he states. "We not only prospered in our own souls here as a church but we had a continuous revival or were in what might be properly regarded as a revival state. Our students were converted by scores and the Lord overshadowed us continually with clouds of His mercy. Gales of divine influence swept over us from year to year producing abundantly the fruits of the Spirit. I have always attributed our success in this good work entirely to the grace of God."

This revival spirit marked the college during Finney's life and ministry. Even after the new buildings were completed and some of the early struggles were passed was this true. In 1850, while the evangelist was holding revivals in England, he sent home a request asking his people to pray that God's blessings would rest mightily upon him. While the students and others were praying for him a revival broke out in their midst and three hundred were converted before it was over.

A year or so after his return from abroad another revival swept the college and from the converts a hundred and five new members were received into the church at one time. In 1866-67 came the "great revival" which reached an unusually large number of business men in the city as well as students.

In 1851 when Asa Mahan resigned as president of the college, Mr. Finney was elected to fill the position. It is significant that the following year the attendance leaped from 570 to 1020, the greatest increase the school ever enjoyed in so short a time. And except for a period during the Civil War it never fell below the thousand mark. Finney's name as a Christian educator as well as a revivalist was responsible for such marked increase.

He held this post until on August 19, 1865, ill health and advanced age forced him to tender his resignation to the trustees, which however was not acted upon until June, 1866, when a new president was elected to succeed him. During that year much of the work was carried on by members of the faculty, for Finney's impaired health made this necessary.

For this fifteen-year term he thus filled three important positions, president of the college, full-time professor of theology and pastor of the church, either of which was enough for a single individual. But since the revivalist's divine surcharging he never stopped at the mere shouldering of one man's burdens in kingdom enterprises.

The titles as a teacher which Mr. Finney held changed with the years, though doubtless the activities and content of his work remained the same. He was elected Professor of Didactic and Polemic Theology February 10, 1835. On August 27, 1840, this was changed to Professor of Theology. Then on August 26, 1851, he became Professor of Theology and Mental and Moral Philosophy. In 1866 his title was changed to Professor of Systematic and Pastoral Theology. Three years later in 1869 his title appeared in the catalog as Professor of Pastoral Theology, which continued to be his title until his death in 1875.

Throughout the term of his presidency he was also ex-officio a member of the Board of Trustees, carrying this grave responsibility along with his administrative work.

From the beginning, colored students sat under Mr. Finney's instruction, one coming with the group of Lane rebels. Shortly afterwards others attended and from 1840 to 1860 the proportion of colored students was between four and five per cent. Oberlin was never intended to be a colored school, but members of that race were admitted on the same terms as white students.

"But the attitude of Oberlin on this subject," writes Beardsley, "and her well-known abolition sympathies created a prejudice against her, a prejudice which was so strong that for four successive years, ending in 1842,

attempts were made in the Ohio legislature to abrogate
the charter of the college."

The devotional side of his teaching was strong. Many
times he would turn his class sessions into prayer meetings when the Spirit overflowed his own soul and spiritually quickened the students. Here is a sample told by
Leonard Parker:

One morning as the end of the term was drawing
near and many of his students were graduating, Finney
opened his class with the usual devotional period, but
"soon the great deep of his heart was broken up, and
he poured out a mighty stream of supplication for the
class, for his former colaborers, for the ministry, for
the church bought with Jesus' blood. Sometimes he
seemed to be leading us; again he seemed to be alone
with God . . . We remained on our knees a whole hour,
and then rose and went silently to our rooms."

This occurred in 1838. On the other hand A. M. Hills,
who sat under Finney's teaching during the latter years
of the revivalist's life, affirms the same thing took place
then, that God broke in upon the class, blessing students
and professor alike.

Finney as an educator saw more to his instruction
than mere head-filling. He looked upon it as heart-
reaching, soul-ennobling, life-changing, and to him education without heart in it was a spiritual failure. Culture
without the Spirit's baptism was impotent to reach a
dying world. He taught that men's lives might be shaped
toward spiritual ends and to attain this goal his teaching
required the same divine illumination as his preaching.

Chapter X

REMARKABLE REVIVALS

The lecture room could not long hold Finney once winter set in, for his soul surged to the throb of evangelism. With him, teaching was a master passion as also was philosophic and dogmatic truth provided they were Spirit baptized and blessed of the Lord. The college trustees had promised him that each winter he would be free to spend his time in revivals, and to this pledge made to his Master he remained true as long as health permitted.

He had builded his fame as an evangelist during the first ten years of his service, but after he became professor at the college, his revival vigor was not to cease. In fact many of his most remarkable revivals came after this time. From Evans Mills to the Broadway Tabernacle is a long leap for ten years' service, but God's direction caused Mr. Finney to make it. Oberlin and the classroom were not an interlude between revivals, rather they became means of extending his evangelism to wider circles.

In 1842 he preached at Boston and then was called to Providence by his friend and benefactor Josiah Chapin, whose yearly contribution of six hundred dollars assisted the evangelist to live. Here he felt he had a love debt to pay.

From the first God's signal blessings were on the meetings until the number of inquirers became so large that the basement room, about the size of the church auditorium, was packed to overflowing. "From night to night," he relates, "that room would be filled with rejoicing converts and trembling, inquiring sinners."

This state of thing continued, he says, for two months. He was tired out, having spent the previous time in Boston in meetings, so he started for home by way of Rochester. Once he was in the city the members of the Bar Association made a written request that he preach a series of sermons to lawyers. He was unaware of the half-skeptical state of mind which existed among them, though there was a "goodly number of pious lawyers" who had been converted in his earlier meeting.

One evening while closing his sermon, he felt a tug at his coat tail and looking around saw a leading Judge, who asked, "Mr. Finney, won't you pray for me by name? and I will take the anxious seat."

"When I announced . . . what he said, it produced a wonderful shock. There was a great gush of feeling . . . The lawyers arose *en masse* and crowded into the aisles, and filled the open space in front, wherever they could get a place to kneel."

One day as he went into the service, a lawyer met him at the door and handing him a paper said, "I deliver this to you as the servant of the Lord Jesus Christ." When he examined it he found it to be a quit-claim deed, made out properly and executed rightly, in which he "quit-claimed to the Lord Jesus Christ all ownership of himself and of everything he possessed."

When asked how he promoted this revival, Finney answered, "The measures were simply preaching the gospel and abundant prayer . . . much stress being always laid upon prayer as an essential means of promoting a revival."

Several of the lawyers converted in this revival entered the ministry, many of whom gained remarkable success.

Thirteen years later in 1855 Finney was again invited to preach in Rochester where once more many striking conversions took place. In this meeting merchants arranged to have their clerks attend the day services. "This became so general throughout the city that in all places of public resort, in stores and public houses, in banks, in the street and in public conveyances and everywhere, the work of salvation that was going on was the absorbing topic," he states.

The soul-saving work continued until "it seemed as if the whole city would be converted."

The following winter, 1843, found him in Boston, the heart of Universalism and Unitarianism. Beecher said to him, "Mr. Finney, you cannot labor here as you do anywhere else. You have to pursue a different course . . . the foundations of Christianity have fallen away."

This is the evangelist's answer: "During the winter the Lord gave my own soul a very thorough overhauling and a fresh baptism of His Spirit. My mind was greatly drawn out in *prayer* . . . My mind was exercised on the question of personal holiness.

"I gave myself to a great deal of *prayer*. I rose at four o'clock in the morning . . . and engaged in *prayer*. I frequently *prayed* till . . . eight o'clock . . . I spent a long time *upon my knees* considering the matter all over and giving up everything to the will of God.

"Holiness to the Lord seemed to be inscribed on all the exercises of my mind . . . I often found myself smiling as it were in the face of God and saying that I did not want anything."

This was what Finney needed to lay siege to the source of intellectual doubt and spiritual degeneracy. This soul overhauling, as he expressed it, and this fresh baptism with the Spirit furnished him with a revitalized approach to the old problems of doubt. Here he found that when the heart was warmed with the fires of conviction and thoroughly awakened by conversion doubts as expressed by skeptics and Unitarians disappeared. So to have a revival in Boston, he merely kindled anew the holy fires that burned in his soul. This enkindling proved contagious and others caught it.

A few years after this refreshing in 1847 his wife died, "in a heavenly state of mind." At first he was overcome with grief, but when the Spirit spoke, he knew she was in heaven.

"It seemed," he wrote, "that I could enter into the very state of mind in which she was in heaven, and if there is any such thing as communing with an absent spirit or with one who is in heaven, I seemed to commune with her."

For many years Finney had been receiving calls from England where his *Revival Lectures* prepared the way for him. In the autumn of 1849 the Spirit led him to accept these calls. His first meeting was at Houghton, where the revival "commenced immediately, attracting people from a distance of forty miles." The same soul-winning success marked his Birmingham revival where often the churches were filled to overflowing and the inquiry rooms packed with anxious seekers.

In these meetings he was assisted greatly by his second wife, Mrs. Elizabeth Atkinson of Rochester. Her presence in the services enhanced his work.

While preaching at Worcester he received a call to hold a meeting for Dr. John Campbell, editor of the *British Banner* and pastor of the Whitefield Tabernacle in London. He began these meetings in May, 1850, preaching as he usually did to those Londoners "to convict the people of sin as deeply and as universally as possible." After preaching for several weeks in this vein he saw it was time to call seekers.

"Have you a room," he asked the pastor, "to which I can invite inquirers after preaching?" The doctor answered that there was the infant room, seating "about thirty or forty." "That is not half large enough," responded Finney and asked for a larger one.

Down the street a ways around a bend in the road was a school room, seating fifteen or sixteen hundred, "and of course you don't want that," said the minister.

"That's the very room," came the evangelist's quick answer.

After preaching that night Finney exhorted those who wanted to find the Lord as their Redeemer to meet him for an inquiry meeting in the schoolroom. For fear he might be misunderstood as to whom he wanted to be there, he said, "Professors of religion are not invited to attend this meeting . . . Careless sinners are not invited . . . Those and those only are expected to attend who are not Christians, but who are anxious for the salvation of their souls."

He repeated his instructions, not wanting to fill the building with curiosity seekers. And of course doubting Campbell "looked out the window to see which way the congregation went." He needn't however, for Finney had heard from God!

Campbell himself estimated that there were no less than fifteen or sixteen hundred seekers on their knees at that meeting! "After I had laid the gospel net thoroughly around them, I prepared to draw it ashore," says Finney. The aisles in the house were so narrow and packed that it was impossible to use the anxious seat. Every seat and every spot became a mourners' bench.

Many times during the months that were to follow this continued, and Finney said he saw as many as two thousand on their knees at a time seeking the Lord.

After a short trip to France to recuperate his strength, he returned to his college duties which called him in May, 1851. But college problems could only hold his attention during the summer and fall, and when winter set in, Finney was again in the evangelistic harness. This time he went to Hartford where Bushnell was pastor and was in the throes of a theological controversy because of his unsound doctrine of the atonement.

He also was then laying the framework for his doctrine of Christian training which eliminated the necessity of a child's being converted. Finney left these dogmatic discussions to others, trusting that time would solve them. He got the spiritually minded people praying.

"In this revival," he says, "there was a great deal of praying. The young converts gave themselves to much prayer." They organized a praying band, finally to crowd out the room in the home where they were invited for their prayer service. These meetings multiplied until a number of them were held in different homes each night after preaching. Under such conditions God could but give the evangelist souls.

Mrs. Finney's meetings for ladies were greatly used for the salvation of women, a work which God led her into while in London.

The following winter, after a siege in the lecture room, found the evangelist in Syracuse "where there was a great movement among the dry bones," and conversions "were multiplied on every side."

Each spring he would return to his classwork at Oberlin and then in the winter he held revivals in whatever places God seemed to direct. In the winter of 1854-55 he went back to his early scene of labor at Western and Rome. A new generation had grown up since his first revival at those places. God used the evangelist remarkably at Western. In this revival he was led to preach on restitution and covering sins.

Shortly after the sermon many cases of restitution came to his attention. After telling about young women restoring clothes they had stolen and young men making restitutions for their frauds, he says, "It seemed as if the word of the Lord was sent home with such power at that time in that city as to uncover a very den of wickedness."

The winter of 1855 found Finney again in Rochester, to be called the following winter to Boston. He began his labors in the Park Street Congregational Church, where his first sermon was directed toward awakening the church to the necessity of a revival. He said, "I always began by trying to stir up a thorough and pervading interest among the professors of religion to secure the reclaiming of those that were backslidden and search out those that were self-deceived, and if possible, bring them to Christ."

The work of salvation was extensive and when time came to leave in the spring he promised to return in the fall to continue the revival. That winter, 1857-58, was the time of the great prayer revival that stirred the Northern States.

It started in a prayer meeting in the Fulton Street Dutch Reformed Church in New York City where Joseph Lanipher began praying for a revival. From there it spread throughout the city, leaped to other cities, took Philadelphia, reached to Boston.

Such prayer meetings were established throughout all the Northern States. "I recollect," says Finney, "in one of our prayer meetings in Boston that winter a gentleman arose and said, 'I am from Omaha, Nebraska. On my journey east I have found a continuous prayer meeting about two thousand miles in extent.'"

The Lord began a general sweep of Boston from a noon prayer meeting in Old South Church. Daily prayer meetings were established in other parts of the city. Mrs. Finney's prayer meetings for ladies held daily at the Park Street Church were crowded. Finney preached throughout the city and everywhere souls were converted by the hundreds, until all count of converts was lost track of.

"A divine influence," affirms the evangelist, "seemed to pervade the whole land . . . It (the revival) was carried on very much through the instrumentality of prayer meetings and personal efforts. The ministers did not oppose it; but the general impression seemed to be, 'We have had instruction enough until we are hardened; it is time for us to pray.' In answer to prayer the windows of heaven were opened and the Spirit of God poured out like a flood."

Newspapers in New York City and elsewhere devoted whole issues to the revival news. During the first year of the revival it was estimated that five hundred thousand souls had been converted, and a million before the revival ran its prayer-shaped course.

While Finney was preaching in Boston during this time, Theodore Parker, the Unitarian preacher, did all in his power to block the revival wheels. Finney sought a private conversation with him but was denied this privilege. Many people, deeply convicted under Finney's preaching, would go to the Music Hall and listen to Parker and lose their sense of impending soul doom.

Finney knew but one way so solve the problem . . . the prayer-way. Forty Christians met in the vestry of the Park Street Church and prayed for God to overcome the evil being done by the Unitarian divine. They prayed until they obtained the witness.

"I have it," cried one man, "God hears our prayers!"

From that hour the tide changed. Parker became sick and fled from the city to Europe in search of health, which he could not find. He never again returned to Boston, for he died in Florence!

"Persons from all evangelical denominations," writes Edwin Lamson in a letter which was read at the Finney Memorial Convention held in Oberlin, July 28, 1876, "were so strongly of one mind that it was agreed by them to set apart a day for special prayer that God would either convert Theodore Parker . . . or in some way destroy his influence so that sinners would no more stumble by reason of his teachings. It was a day long to be remembered."

Lamson was one of those who prayed. God, Finney was able to say, still hears and answers prayer.

God had yet one other year of mighty soul winning for him before these strenuous labors should be laid aside. That winter of evangelism, 1858-59, was to be spent in England.

"The church and ministry in this country," he affirms, "had become so very extensively engaged in promoting the revival and such was the blessing of God attending the exertions of laymen as well as of ministers, that I made up my mind to return and spend another season in England, and see if the same influence would not pervade that country."

That proved to be a profitable season of evangelism. He makes such statements of the work as these: "I spent several weeks laboring in Houghton and Saint Ives, where we saw precious revivals. In Saint Ives they had never had a revival before . . . The revival took powerful effect there."

His next sphere of service was London, where "the Spirit of God was poured out . . . in a state of great conviction." Of the Huntington meeting he says, "It greatly changed the religious aspect of the town."

After laboring in London the revivalist accepted a call to work with a Dr. Kirk of the Evangelical Union Church in Edinburgh, Scotland, which denomination was the result of a revival that broke out through reading Finney's *Revival Lectures*. Here victories were won on their knees and souls were awakened to their spiritual possibilities in Christ. From Edinburgh he was called by a minister of the same denomination to labor in Aberdeen, where a gracious revival swept the city.

It was, however, at Bolton, one of Wesley's fields of labor, where his greatest soul victories were won. Here the revival continued for three months. Finney as usual got the Christians praying and working in the city. He recommended that they visit two by two every house in the city, and where possible pray in every one. "They immediately and courageously rallied to perform this work," he notes.

The city became awakened and he says that if their building would have seated so large a number there would have been ten thousand in attendance at the services. In one afternoon in a cotton mill sixty workmen were brought into a joyous relation to Christ.

After preaching on confession and restitution one evening a man from the congregation restored seventy-five hundred dollars to a person whom he had wronged to that amount. Another person made restitution to the amount of thirty thousand dollars.

After this meeting came Manchester, where Finney, Oberlin's President (at least during the summertime and God's great soul winner during the winter) received many letters requesting him to return. He was now sixty-eight years old, and for nearly forty years he had been performing prodigious tasks, actually doing the work of several men. There had been a growing sentiment at Oberlin that he need not longer expect revivals during school terms.

With these sentiments in his mind, he and his wife turned their faces toward the college in the woods. He went home from one of the most powerful revivals he had ever witnessed to take a slight cold which was followed by a three months' sickness.

He was disturbed in his own mind over the growing feeling which Oberlin was manifesting. He says: "I saw that an impression seemed to be growing in Oberlin that during term time we could not expect a revival and that our revivals must be expected to occur during the long vacations in the winter . . . But I had come to Oberlin and resided here for the sake of the students to secure their conversion and sanctification."

In answering this growing sentiment, he said that if this was going to be the prevalent idea, Oberlin was not the place for him. "I was free in saying that unless there could be a change, Oberlin was not my field of labor any longer."

This England trip was the last of Finney's evangelistic tours. "Since 1860," he relates, "although continually pressed by churches . . . to come and labor as an evangelist, I have not dared comply with their requests . . . I have felt inadequate to the exposure and labor of attempting to secure revivals abroad."

Oberlin, however, was refreshed by several revivals before Finney's death. In 1866-67 revival fires again blazed grandly in the college. Here is Finney's last report of a meeting:

"Thus I have brought my revival narrative down to this time, the 13th of January, 1868. Yesterday, Sabbath, we had a very solemn day in the First church. I preached all day upon resisting the Holy Ghost. At the close of the afternoon service, I called upon all the professors of religion to rise up and unite with us in prayer . . . We then had a very solemn season of prayer."

Two or three years later Dr. A. M. Hills, then a ministerial student under Finney, says, "I saw on a Sabbath afternoon one hundred people, mostly students, come down out of the gallery and gather before the pulpit to be prayed for and give themselves to God, though there had not been an extra religious service in the town. It was only the climax of a series of sermons by Finney, all purposely bearing toward that end."

Thus practically to the close of this magnificent life the one plea of Finney was for souls. At this time he was well past the seventy-five mark, but this man who had won his hundreds of thousands in other men's pulpits could not go to his grave without having the knowledge that his own pulpit and his own church were likewise the scene of spiritual outpourings. He wanted the last shouts that echoed through the corridors of his fading memory as earth receded and heaven came near to be shouts of new-born souls.

CHAPTER XI

MARVELOUS CONVERSIONS AND UNUSUAL FAITH

Connected with Finney's revivals were many remarkable conversions. When the divine light broke into his own soul it came with unusual glory and power, and in his meetings such experiences were to be duplicated. God, however, had a work for him to do that set him apart from others in the consequences of his life's labors. Many times deep conviction fell upon his audiences until individuals would weep and groan as though they were about to die. They were, as Finney said, dying to the world's call, the power of evil in their lives that they might be raised up with Christ in the newness of divine life.

While Finney was preaching at Rome, deep awe filled the town and the Spirit's convicting power was mightily upon the people. Deluges of Pentecost literally swept through the city, ebbing and flowing in and out of the church into homes, onto the streets, flooding hotels, stores, banks and schools. Came the sheriff from Utica to the meeting. Finney tells the story thus:

"The state of things in the village and in the neighborhood round about was such that no one could come into the village without feeling awe-stricken with the impression that God was there in a peculiar and wonderful manner. The sheriff of the county resided at Utica. There were two courthouses in the county, one at Rome and the other at Utica. He afterwards told me that he heard of the state of things at Rome and he together with others had a good deal of laughing *in the hotel* where he boarded about what they had heard."

That same hotel, then a scene of mockery, was to be turned into a center of holy revival fires before the meeting in Utica came to a close.

"One day," Finney goes on to relate, "it was necessary for him to go to Rome. He wanted to see for himself what it was that people talked so much about and what the state of things really was in Rome. He drove on in his one horse sleigh without any particular impression upon his mind at all, until he crossed the old canal, a place about a mile from the town."

Crossing the canal he was suddenly confronted with a divine sense of impending spiritual doom which settled like a pall over his soul and darkened his mind. It was "an awe so deep that he could not shake it off." He felt as if the whole atmosphere was pervaded with God. The nearer he came to the town the heavier seemed the cloud of divine presence.

Coming to the hotel, when the hostler took away his horse, it seemed to the sheriff that the man looked just like he himself felt, "as if he were afraid to speak." They sensed the near presence of God as though they stood at the long-ago Sinai scene and heard the divine Voice and its thunders and rumbling shaking the mountain.

Finding the man with whom he had business, he could not attend to it, for "they all were manifestly so much impressed that they could hardly attend to business."

At the table the sheriff had to leave abruptly and go to the window "to divert his attentions and keep from weeping. He observed that everybody else appeared to feel just as he did. Such an awe, such a solemnity, such a state of things, he had never had any conception of before."

He didn't attend the meeting, but returned to Utica. Never again did he make mockery of divine things nor laugh at Finney's revivals.

Shortly when the meetings were moved to Utica the sheriff came to the services one evening. Finney took his text, spoke a few moments, and then noticed the sheriff "turn deliberately around, wrap his great coat about him and kneel down. The sheriff continued on his knees during the whole service."

Retiring to his hotel room, he treasured in his mind the sermon, and said to his soul, "My soul, will you accept Christ, give up sin and give up yourself? And will you do it now?" He emphasized the "now and here" of acceptance as he lay across his bed. "Right there his distress left him so suddenly that he fell asleep, and did not wake for several hours. When he did awake, he found his mind full of peace and rest in Christ. From this moment he became an earnest worker for Christ among his acquaintances."

Soon he led the hotel keeper to the Master. "The Spirit took powerful hold in that house . . . Indeed that largest hotel in the town became a center of spiritual influence and many were converted there. The stages as they passed through stopped at the hotel, and so powerful was the impression in the community that I heard of several cases of persons that just stopped for a meal, or to spend a night, being powerfully convicted and converted before they left the town."

It was the common remark that nobody could be in this place or in Rome during the time or pass through either without "being aware of the presence of God; that a divine influence seemed to pervade the place and the whole atmosphere to be instinct with a divine life."

In Philadelphia later another marvelous conversion occurred. A woman, whose husband was an infidel, was gloriously converted after facing her husband's threats that she must not attend the Finney meetings. She asked Finney for his opinion and he said, "He is an infidel and his opinions on religious subjects are not to be respected."

"She soon came into the liberty of the Gospel, had great faith and peace of mind and enjoyed the presence of God. This highly displeased her husband and he finally went so far as to threaten her life if she went to meeting again."

She had seen him so often in a rage that she did not doubt he would carry out his threat. In light of this she obeyed the heavenly surcharging and went.

"When she returned from meeting she found him in great rage. As soon as she entered the door he locked it and took out the key and then he drew a dagger and swore that he would take her life. She ran up the stairs. He caught a light to follow her, but the servant girl blew out the light as he passed by her. This left them both in the dark."

From one room to the other, up stairs and down, into the kitchen and to the cellar she went. While he with his drawn dagger was stumbling through the darkness to slit her heart, she drug herself out of the cellar window and escaped to stay all night with a friend.

Returning home she thought he would have appeased his conscience and leave her alone. She found the house torn upside down, furniture broken and things in disorder. He met her at the door, locked it and drawing his dagger, "he threw himself upon his knees and held up his hands and took the most horrible oath that he would there take her life."

In astonishment she looked at him and fled. The race began again and this time in the light. Up the stairs she sped only to be followed by the dagger-carrying maniac. She went from room to room seeking an escape but none. Finally he cornered her.

"She threw herself upon her knees as he was about to strike her with his dagger and lifted up her hands to heaven and cried for mercy upon herself and upon him.

"At this point *God arrested him*. He looked at her for a moment, dropped the dagger, and fell upon the floor and cried for mercy himself. He then and there broke down, confessed his sins to God and to her, and begged God and her to forgive him."

Great peace swept through the fire-burned regions of his inner nature and he arose a God-changed man. From then on he was an earnest Christian, laboring to bring others to the fellowship of Christ which had so marvelously transformed him . . .

During Finney's first Buffalo meeting God gave him an unusual case of conviction and conversion through a wealthy and influential lawyer. One of the interesting things in these meetings was the fact that God was no respector of persons as to the types of people reached. Some were from society's highest strata, others from the lowest dregs of humanity. In this case it was a skeptical lawyer who "rebelled decidedly against the teachings of the revival." Finney in his sermons specialized on the lawyer's needs.

"I hunted him from his refuges," relates the evangelist, "and answered all his objections and met all his excuses."

The man became mentally upset and excited, declaring that he would not believe such teachings. God's Spirit worked upon his soul while Finney worked upon his mind. "I did not hesitate," he says, "to press him in every sermon, in one shape or another with his unwillingness to be a Christian."

One evening he sat across from a notorious scoffer who, as Finney's sermon points were driven home with sledgehammer logic, would look across the aisle and smile as if to say, "We don't believe him, do we?" This riled the lawyer for he did not want to be typed with such low-class doubters. He felt himself above them in intellectual genius and he wanted to measure his doubting in a larger cup than held theirs.

Finney that night pressed sinners' consciences so hard to accept *now* and *willingly* come to Christ that the lawyer could not contain himself. When the meeting was over the aisle was so crowded that people pressed against the lawyer with such force that he openly swore. His wife feared that he was grieving God's Spirit away.

Going home he could not sleep and finally went out into a near-by grove where he could pray aloud and lift the burden that stoned-down his heart. But to his mortification and surprise he found he could not pray.

"He had no words; he had no desires that he could express in words. His heart was as hard as marble and he had not the least feeling on the subject. He stood upon his knees disappointed and confounded, and found that if he opened his mouth to pray he had nothing in the form of prayer that he could sincerely utter."

He decided to try the Lord's Prayer, so he began, saying, "Our Father . . . " But was stopped and convicted for his hypocrisy in calling God his Father. "Hallowed be they name . . . " he tried once more, only to be shocked, for he knew he did not hold God's name hallowed.

"Thy kingdom come . . . " he went on. But he knew he did not want the kingdom to come and the words almost choked him. "Thy will be . . . " But he did not want God's will to be done and his heart rose up against it, "and he could not say it. Here he was brought face to face with the will of God . . . He had been told that he was opposed to this will . . . But here on his knees, with the Lord's prayer in his mouth, he was brought face to face with that question; and he saw with perfect clearness that what he had been told was true, that he was not willing that God's will should be done."

Here was the whole question of his rebellion and it was brought so forcefully to confront him that he saw he must give up his willing opposition to God's divine course in his life. "And then he gathered up all the strength of his will and cried aloud, 'Thy will be done on earth as it is in heaven.' He was perfectly conscious that his will went with his words; that he accepted the will of God and the whole will of God; that he made a full surrender to God and accepted Christ just as he was offered in the Gospel. He gave up his sins and embraced the will of God as his universal rule of life."

Peace brooded over his submitted soul and his rebellion passed away. "His feelings subsided into a great calm and a sweet peace seemed to fill all his soul." From then on he became an earnest worker and later gave to God a son for the ministry.

While these conversions were remarkable in that God swept away opposition and finally ruled supreme in their souls, others hardened themselves in their resistance to the Holy Spirit and were struck dead. Many such instances are noted in Finney's Memoirs, of which the following is a sample.

"But in this revival (at Rome) as in others that I have known," says the evangelist, "God did some terrible things in righteousness."

There were three men who resisted continually the call of God during this meeting. They would have none of the revivalist's salvation nor would they listen to the call of the divine. The atmosphere of the meeting was so charged with an awe-striking divine presence, as noted in the story of the sheriff's conversion, that men could not escape the sense that the Almighty was confronting them.

These three men were driven to desperation in their attempt to run away from the Spirit's warning call. On one particular Sunday when the meeting had reached a high tide of convicting terribleness, these men decided to drown their soul disturbances in a drinking bout. They would drink themselves insensible and then God could not warn them.

"They spent the day in drinking and ridiculing the work of God," says Finney. "They went on in this way until one of them suddenly fell dead."

Said the minister, "There! there is no doubt but that man has been stricken down by God and has been sent to hell. "

The dead man's companions were speechless. They could say nothing; for it was evident to them that their conduct had brought upon him "this awful stroke of divine indignation."

Finney met many unusual instances of faith during his long course of evangelism. He marked his work with great prayer, feeling that unless he could pray through himself and could lead the people to pray through, no revival would be possible. In this way he developed bands of praying folk that would go to all limits to see divine glory flood their city. He tells of one woman in Syracuse whom he met in 1851, who was notable for her faith.

She was known as Mother Austin and was a dependent widow, who was literally fed by the folk of the city. She said once to Finney, "Brother Finney, it is impossible for me to suffer for any of the necessities of life, because God has said to me, 'Trust in the Lord and do good: so shalt thou dwell in the land and verily thou shalt be fed.' "

Says the revivalist, "Indeed it was notorious through the city, as far as I could learn, that Mother Austin's faith was like a bank; and that she never suffered for want of the necessities of life, because she drew on God."

She was an uneducated person, but by sinner and Christian alike she was regarded as a saint. Finney says he never witnessed a case of greater simplicity in faith than she manifested. In a remarkable manner God literally fed her day by day. Here is one of many instances:

"She said, one Saturday evening a friend of hers, but an impenitent man, called to see her, and after conversing awhile he offered her . . . a five dollar bill. She said that she felt an inward admonition not to take it. She felt that God definitely warned her not to take it

. . . that it would be an act of self-righteousness on the part of the man and might do him more harm than it would do her good."

She declined the money and the man went away, though she knew she had only enough wood and food to last her over the Sabbath, and she had no means of obtaining any more. Still she was not afraid to trust in God "as she had done for so many years."

Sunday broke with a violent snowstorm, and by Monday the snow was several feet deep and the blocked street made assistance impossible. On that day she and her young son found themselves snowed in. Asked the boy, "Mother, what shall we have for breakfast?" They had been able to muster up enough wood for a tiny fire. "I do not know, my son; but the Lord will provide."

The boy began to weep as she looked out and saw it was impossible for any assistance to get through to them. However she began to make preparation for the morning meal, setting the table, "believing that some would come in due season."

"Very soon," narrates Finney, "she heard a loud talking in the streets and went to the window to see what it was, and beheld a man in a single sleigh, and some men with him shoveling the snow so that the horse could get through. Up they came to her door and behold! they had brought her a plenty of fuel and provision, everything to make her comfortable for several days."

Nor did Finney leave all the praying for small necessities to others. He gave himself mightily to prayer for his revivals, often arising at four in the morning, praying during the forenoon hours, and even all night.

Here is a sample of how the man confronted God with his petitions:

During the summer of 1853 Oberlin was struck with a severe drought. The hay fields were dried up so there was no feed for the cattle. The cattle soon must die and the harvest fail *unless rain comes*. Crops had withered, wells dried up, and the parched earth became powdery.

On Sunday morning the church was filled. Not a cloud was in sight and no one expected a drop of water to fall from the skies that day. The situation was desperate. Finney arose from his chair walked to the pulpit and lifted his voice in prayer.

"O Lord! send us rain. We pray for rain. Our harvests perish. There is not a drop for the thirsting birds. The ground is parched. The choking cattle lift their voices toward a brassy heaven and lowing, cry 'Lord give us water' . . . We do not presume to dictate to Thee what is best for us, yet Thou dost invite us to come to Thee as children to a father and tell Thee all our wants. *We want rain!* Even the squirrels in the woods are suffering for want of it. Unless Thou givest us rain our cattle must die . . . *O Lord, send us rain! and send it now!* for Jesus sake! Amen!" *

"In the preacher's voice," reports the California minister, "was the plaintiveness of a creature's cry. I do not know whether any pencil caught more of this won-

---

* This prayer is related by two different individuals, both eye witnesses, one Rev. Joseph Adams in *Reminiscences of Charles Finney* and the other an Oberlin student, later to become a California minister, who reports it in the *Advocate*, and is quoted by Henrietta Matson, in her *Recollections of Charles G. Finney.*

derful prayer, but all who heard it had to tell of its
bold importunity. It had the pathos and power of an
Isaiah."

Then the pastor-revivalist poured out his soul in a
searching sermon, "hewing close to the line," from the
text, "I have somewhat against thee because thou hast
left thy first love."

"Not many minutes did the sermon go on before a
cloud about the size of a man's hand came athwart the
summer sky," says the California preacher, "It grew
fast. The wind rattled the shutters of the old church.
Darkness came on the air, joy aroused our anxious hearts
as great raindrops pattered on the sun-scorched shingles
of the monumental old church."

Finney's lithe figure, tall as a Sioux warrior, ruddy
as a David, trembled. His clarion voice choked. God
had heard his cry. The sermon was never finished, for
torrents of water poured from the prayer-unlocked
heavens. The preacher bowed over the pulpit and said,
"Let us thank the Lord for the rain."

He gave out the hymn,

When all they mercies, O my God,
My rising soul surveys,
Transported with the view, I'm lost
In wonder, love and praise.

The congregation could not sing for weeping. Then
Finney lifted heavenward a prayer of thanksgiving and
praise. "I can remember not a word of the closing
prayer, but the reverent and relaxed figure, the
pathetic voice, the pallid and awe-struck countenance,
are vivid as if it were yesterday; the plank sidewalks
of the dear old town splashed our garments as we
walked home from a very short service, of which life's

memory must be lasting." This is the testimony of the
student who sat in the gallery and saw and heard Finney
that morning.

Nor did the outpoured rain close the story of those
opened heavens. That afternoon the congregation packed
the building once again, so the minister "could comfort
the slain of the Lord."

"I have never witnessed so solemn a scene," says the
minister in his *Advance* story. "He continued with added
force and directness until his shafts struck home . . .
From the galleries, the side seats and the choir they filed
solemnly to the front seats. If the old church seats
fifteen hundred, then there were a thousand penitents
at her altar that day."

Among the weeping throng an impressive black man
arose way in the back of the audience to speak. Said an
usher to Finney, "Fredrick Douglass has something to
say to the people."

The great colored orator, now gray-haired and form-
bent, came forward for forgiveness. He said, "When
I was young and a slave, Mr. Finney, when my back
quivered under the master's lash, I clung close to God
and felt the comfort of true religion. But prosperity has
been too much for me, and I have come under the
dominion of the world, and have lost my first love."

Finney, the soul-stirred preacher, wept aloud and
cried, "God bless you, Brother Douglass! God bless
you!" So the evangelist comforted his colored brother.

This was the Finney God had called to a field of
world evangelism and had endowed him with childlike
faith, a faith that could pull back the brassy heavens,
unlock heaven's gates and flood both earth and men's
souls with heavenly waters.

Chapter XII

EVEN DOWN TO OLD AGE

The glory of Finney's life and the power of his spiritual vigor did not diminish with old age. Age served to mellow his experience of divine contacts. He said, "I want you to live so near the river of life that you drink fresh draughts daily . . . " This desire for his converts issued from his own life as Christ's indwelling filled him, for what he preached he first lived.

"All through my acquaintance with him," affirms George Clark, an Oberlin student, "it was a mystery to me where he got his mighty power. It seemed to be always gushing up, always full. That mystery was solved when I read his Memoirs. It was God in him that made him so great a blessing."

This God-in-him experience enlarged and increased as he neared the end of his life. Physical energy declined but spiritual stamina became greater with advanced age. Those who came in contact with him during the latter days of his life affirm they saw in him an ever-flourishing spiritual intensity.

In 1860 he ceased his evangelistic travels with his return from England. He decided that he must give up either his teaching and pastorate at Oberlin or his outside evangelism. He chose Oberlin as the closing scenes of his ministry. Nor was he inactive during that time though he was within two years of the alloted days of man, three score and ten.

One of the great privileges of his teaching ministry was his Thursday sermon, a custom which he began when he first moved to the college and which continued as long as he was alive. During these latter years he kept up this practice, though at times he was forced to be assisted by other speakers. In these meetings he was more or less didactic, which sprang from his classroom method.

"It was in his sermons upon the Sabbath," writes G. Fredrick Wright, "and upon Thursday afternoons that one would hear his most complete and effective presentation of the great themes of the gospel. His pupils ever prized these occasions as an indispensable supplement to their classroom exercises."

Doubtless his greatest influence exerted upon the students who did not attend his class instruction came from these sermons. They possibly wrought more for the Master than his formal instruction. "So prominent was the doctrinal element in his preaching . . . that scarcely any of the twenty thousand students who from time to time came statedly under his ministrations failed to get the salient points of his theology," says his first biographer.

Meanwhile he not only preached on Sundays and Thursdays, as well as taught his classes in Pastoral Theology, but he carried the heavy burdens of a college president. This triple work continued until his resignation, as noted above, from the administrative duties as president in 1866.

In 1863 the shadow of a tragedy hung again over his home due to the death of his second wife. Sometime later he married the third time, the lady being Rebecca A. Rayl, who had been the assistant principal in the ladies department of the college. She outlived him by thirty-two years.

His pen that had been active so many years had built a world-wide audience for his messages. He had begun writing during the earlier years of his ministry and continued even to the end of his life. In all he wrote seventeen books for publication, four of which remain alive until today, these being his *Revival Lectures, Lectures to Professing Christians, Memoirs* and *Systematic Theology.* His *Revival Lectures* rank among the best religious classics in the number of sales.

This book alone was sufficient to assure Finney a place in the halls of fame through all Christian centuries. On the subject there is no other book that stands as its equal. As long as revivals shall be held and men seek to kindle revival fires this book will be read. The book was forged in the furnace of Christian experience and was written not as intellectual theories. The messages were revival ground-work in print.

After retiring as president Finney wrote a book entitled *Free Masonry,* in 1869, in which he set forth the anti-Christian nature of Masonry. He had been a member of the order before conversion and attended a meeting or so after he met God. It seemed to him that he was out of place in such an environment so he withdrew from membership. The year previous he finished his *Memoirs,* though they were not printed until after his death. The year following his death a book of sermons was published, the title being *Sermons on Gospel Themes.*

1891 appeared a posthumous volume of sermons called *Sermons on the Way of Salvation.* His book *Views of Sanctifiation,* which came out in 1840, was later enlarged and added in essence to his *Systematic Theology* so that he might give in a more extended manner his views on the doctrine of consecration and Christian holiness.

The National Congregational Council, meeting in Oberlin in 1871, asked Finney to address them on "The Gift of the Holy Spirit." The weight of his seventy-nine years was heavy upon him, but his mind soon took fire with the vigor of his yester-years and he kindled to the theme on which he had preached so many times. His clear voice filled the auditorium and with divine unction he carried the audience along with him. Those who heard him say that his face was bathed in tears as he proclaimed the doctrine which had been the heart of his evangelism.

The following year he laid down the heavy burden of being pastor of the college and town church, a love service he had carried since 1836. Though he resigned as stated pastor, his preaching did not cease at that time. Now eighty, it seemed that another's shoulders should be slipped under these ministerial burdens. A. M. Hills heard him preach during that last summer of his pastorate, the year of his own graduation from Oberlin, and as this veteran evangelist arose and announced his texts from Sunday to Sunday the logic of the Gospel was set on fire and his messages became radiant with divine truth.

As a pastor he was a true shepherd of his flock, attending faithfully to the spiritual functions of his office. Besides his Sunday sermons, he led the midweek prayer meeting and held an inquiry meeting at sometime during each week. When asked to counsel a soul in the throes of need, he never lagged in his duty. Where sickness called, Finney was there. During these last pastoral years he often walked for miles to visit the sick and dying that he might administer spiritual comfort to them. "His presence," affirms Mr. Wright, "in the sick room was as gentle as that of a woman."

Dr. James Brand was chosen as Finney's successor as pastor of the church. When he preached his first sermon in the evangelist's presence, he was naturally very nervous, but the next morning he met Finney who dissolved all sense of fear from his mind.

"A more genial, tender, sympathetic, childlike character," he says, "I had never met . . . During the two remaining years of his life, though still living among a people who idolized him, and to whom his word was law, he never . . . offered a suggestion or made a criticism . . . He always sent me away a wiser man and with deeper longing to win men to Christ . . . "

His wish to be freed from all "further pastoral responsibility and care" was finally granted. The committee, appointed to express appreciation for his services, made mention of the following elements in his pastoral work:

"Your consistent and blameless Christian life, a delightful and ever-shining example of the grace of our blessed Lord.

"Your tender sympathy with every individual member of the church, especially with the sick and the afflicted.

"Your ceaseless, zealous, and effectual efforts for the salvation of sinners, your wise conversation with inquirers after Christ . . .

"Your fervid and pungent sermons, wrought out through much believing prayer and faithful intelligent study of God's word . . .

"Your labors and prayers for the Church universal, your revival efforts abroad, your published letters and books, all breathing the same spirit of love and power which has characterized your Christian activity at home."

These were words which resounded from every person who came under this man's mighty soul-elevating ministry.

Finney's theme during these latter years was that of the aged Apostle John . . . love. He could hardly refer to God's sweep of divine love without his cheeks being stained with tears.

In his lectures on theology to the students, he often closed the hour with such prayers as this: "Lord mellow their hearts and give life and power to the truth, for if thou dost not, their sermons and theology will be so dry that it would be fit only to choke a moral agent." Again he prayed when closing a class session, "O Lord, do not let these young men think that because they have let down a little line into the infinite sea of Thy greatness they have sounded all its depths."

More often his class prayers were bathed with such pathos and spiritual energizing that the students went from the room with a sense of having been in God's presence. His voice lifted them so near the gates of heaven that they seemed to glimpse therein.

Once he closed a term of school with a prayer that God would give the young ministers a baptism of the Holy Spirit. He asked God not to let them go forth in their own strength to suffer defeat, but to fill them brimming full of the divine. The whole hour was spent in prayer. Said George Clark of that class session which had turned into a prayer meeting, "That was the most profitable lesson I ever learned and the most profitable hour that I ever spent. We came nearer to God, we got a more exalted idea of the work of the ministry, and it was from that scene that I obtained my highest idea of President Finney."

Even to the end he had a princely bearing which always made him a commanding figure among men. The stamp of God was upon his character in the form of gentleness and goodness. His mind, despite his eighty-three years, possessed an alertness which characterized his youthful thinking and speaking. Physically he stood erect as he had always done while in the pulpit.

He completed his last course of lectures to the seminary students not many days before God took him. "It was my privilege to attend one of those lectures only two weeks before he died," writes Henrietta Matson, "and there was the same Holy Ghost unction and power as of old, with perhaps an added sweetness that brought heaven nearer."

He preached each Sunday of his last month on earth, alternating between First Church, which was his old pastorate, and the Second Church. In his last prayer uttered for the congregation he gathered the people whom he loved so dearly to his heart and then commended them to Christ whom he had served so faithfully.

Finney had often expressed a desire to die suddenly and as the end neared he had a growing longing to be away toward his heavenly home. Many times he said, "We thank Thee, Lord, for life, but we shall thank Thee more when we can go home." He lived on the very borders of heaven with only a step to be taken when God's time came.

It was a beautiful Sunday, that August 16, 1875. The sun burst over the hills with a radiant glory that drove back the spheres of night. The birds sang their morning carols which the patriarch noted with tender care.

Late that evening he refrained from attending the service in his beloved near-by church, but the tug on his heart was so intense that he walked out to his gate and stood listening to the glorious refrain which the congregation was singing. His voice was lifted and joined in singing, "Jesus lover of my soul, let me to thy bosom fly . . . "

This was the last earthly song which sprang from the lips of the saint. Retiring to his room he went to bed to be awakened at eleven o'clock with pain ringing his heart. Suffering a few hours, he fell asleep, quietly, restfully, "smiling up into the face of God." And when he awoke it was in the radiant light of heaven's glory. He slept into the arms of Jesus whose messenger he had been for so many glory-crowned years . . .

A simple inscription rests on his pulpit, which reads, "From this pulpit for many years Charles G. Finney presented to this community and to the world the unsearchable riches of Christ." These "unsearchable riches" he had gone home to enjoy.

Oberlin mourned him. The world lost him. But through his ministry of evangelism and teaching thousands have gone forth to tell again to the world the same story which Finney so grandly lived, so dynamically preached. Springing from the inner fount of his own life, he heralded from the pulpit, the lecture room and the press "that Jesus Christ came into the world to save sinners." This was his life-long theme song, this his white-hot passion.

Said President Fairfield to the first graduating class after Finney's death: "Your destiny will be in a measure shaped by what he was and what he did. And here is our relief and satisfaction in closing up such a career of usefulness and power. There is to be no real loss. From that burning and shining light, in which for so long a season we were permitted to rejoice, a thousand other lights have been kindled, and thus the darkness of the world shall be more and more enlightened."

That kindling process, when others' torches have been lighted at his soul fires, goes on today. We are reaching back to him to enkindle the dying embers of evangelism that now smoulder among Christ's followers. May they for us, through his life, burst into flame as he saw them under the power of his personal ministry. Such a man could not die . . . he only sleeps while the glory of his life rides triumphantly on.